THE **COBS CAN!**
WORKBOOK

The author and his mare, Ketchup.

THE **COBS CAN!** WORKBOOK

Progressive Training Exercises for
RIDEABILITY, SUPPLENESS AND **COLLECTION**

OMAR RABIA

J. A. ALLEN

First published in 2016 by J. A. Allen
www.allenbooks.co.uk

J. A. Allen is an imprint of
The Crowood Press Ltd
Ramsbury, Marlborough
Wiltshire SN8 2HR
www.crowood.com

British Library Cataloguing-in-Publication Data
A catalogue record for this book is available from the British Library.

ISBN 978 1 908809 30 8

Illustrations by Carole Vincer

All photographs of the author and his mare, Ketchup, by Karen Burton.
Other photographs, reproduced with permission, are by Berta Images
Photography; Steve Cowling; Chris Etchells; Leanne Robertson;
and Andy Warden.

Disclaimer
The author and publisher shall have neither liability nor responsibility to
any person or entity with respect to any damage or injury caused or alleged
to be caused directly or indirectly by the information contained in this book.
J. A. Allen encourages the use of approved safely helmets in all equestrian
sports and activities.

Designed and Typeset by Paul Saunders
Printed and bound in Malaysia by Times Offset (M) Sdn Bhd

Contents

Acknowledgements

There are so many people to thank, without whom this book would not have been possible. The production of this book would have been impossible without the skills of Karen Burton, who took all the photos of Ketchup and myself, and Martin Diggle, whose diligent editing brought a fresh perspective to my writing, bringing clarity where there was ambiguity and checking for comprehensive detail so that my words cannot be misinterpreted or misunderstood.

I would like to thank all of my regular students for their support and drive, without which a project such as this would not be possible, and those students from further afield whose interaction and enthusiasm for more knowledge stimulate my desire to put my thoughts on paper and promote the virtues of the cob.

A great big thank-you must go to all those riders who provided photos to enrich this book. Thanks to Vicky Strutton for her fabulous photos of herself and her delightful Sound Barrier (or Bill, as he is known at home). Thanks to Mel Sumner for the photos of herself and her lovely cob Billy (who, shortly after she gave me these photos, managed a very good placing at a British Dressage Regional Championships). Thanks to Jane Lavington with her horse Boston, an advanced dressage cob, and her pure-bred Clydesdale, Midge, for fantastic photos illustrating many points so well. And thanks to Tracey Davies for providing two pictures showing her lovely cob Roxy's progress. Thanks also to Lucinda

Stewart for the photos of her riding Leanne Robertson's Clydesdale, Ted, showing that chunkies of all sizes benefit from some more advanced schooling.

A huge thank-you to my family (particularly my mother), who are some of my biggest supporters, keeping me thinking positively and that anything is possible. For his unwavering belief in me, I want to thank Ian, my partner in life and in business; without his faith in my ability with horses, or his support in all areas, I really would be lost. Finally, a huge thank-you to my cobs, my inspiration and my passion – and particularly to Ketchup, my soul-mate and best friend.

Introduction

Since the publication of my first book *Cobs Can!* I have noticed a huge increase in the number of cobs, natives and heavy horses being given more comprehensive schooling, and appearing in classical equitation as well as competitive dressage classes. I would like to think that my book had at least a hand in that and that more 'everyday' riders are enjoying schooling their supposedly 'humble' mounts to a higher level as a result. It became clear, however, that while the book covered each level of schooling and all of the movements, a more progressive, step-by-step guide was necessary for those riders who have not previously had access to this kind of training. Not only did there need to be a step-by-step set of instructions for introducing each movement – there also needed to be a certain amount of guidance on the progression within a certain exercise. For example, a shoulder-in being introduced to a young cob looks very different from a shoulder-in shown by an advanced horse, and it often has a different focus. *The Cobs Can! Workbook* is designed to fill that void. In *Cobs Can!* in-hand groundwork had only a passing mention, but the reality of my practice is that all movements are introduced dismounted first. That discrepancy is addressed in this current book, where guidance is given to develop your cob gymnastically from the ground first. These are the foundations upon which the ridden schooling is built. This book then guides riders through exercises that will perfect their seat in order to train their cob in these movements under saddle. This does not, of course, mean that riders should pay no attention to their seat and posture until their cob's groundwork is advanced! Clearly, no opportunity to improve in these areas should be wasted or delayed. However, in terms of the cob's education and development, this method, which is rooted in classical principles, has clear benefits.

This dual approach to schooling means that, in this text, some exercises and themes are addressed both from a groundwork and a ridden perspective in different chapters, the former appearing in the first section of the book. A comparison of the preparatory groundwork techniques with the techniques employed under saddle will show how the former relate to, and complement, the latter.

As a follow on from *Cobs Can!* this book has been written for the good of the cob and for the good of those riders who choose to travel on their equestrian journey with one of these powerful, kind and gentle horses, whatever their size, conformation or natural movement. In this modern age, where qualified and experienced help from someone with a like-minded philosophy can seem hard to come by, this book, while not replacing training or tuition, will help you on the road to success with these cobs that are so often misunderstood. My aim is to help, to avoid force, to avoid frustration and to engender a sense of enjoyment and success in your equestrian journey.

INTRODUCTION
TO IN-HAND WORK

All of my horses, including my cobs, are schooled through all of the movements in-hand first. This helps in so many ways. We humans are a visual species and during in-hand schooling we can see what is happening and can respond in an instant, whereas ridden work very much depends upon the rider's ability to feel – one of the most elusive skills to learn. Also, working in-hand has the advantage of educating the cob to new movements without him being encumbered by an additional and often unstable weight on his back. It not only builds strength, suppleness and flexibility; it also enhances a sense of calm learning, which will cross over to ridden work. Watching your cob learn through in-hand work also teaches you a lot about your ridden technique and aids, and it helps you to develop that level of feel mentioned above. It is an essential tool in my training kit of skills and helps to avoid the force or heavy-handedness that can often be seen in ridden training alone.

....

CHAPTER ONE

In-Hand Position

Trainer's Position for In-Hand Schooling

In-hand work is not only educational for cob and trainer but also can be honed and polished to the level of art. Just as riding can be brought up to excellence and presented in a polished form, in-hand work can be a way of presenting beauty in equitation where trainer and cob can appear to be partnered-up in a dance hold with seamless movements as they weave around the arena. When watching trainers school their horses in-hand, one notices slight differences – positional as well as postural – that are individual to each trainer and to each horse and trainer partnership. There are, however, a few basic essentials.

Generally speaking, for initial in-hand work the trainer stands close to the shoulder. I would describe that as the default position as, when positioned there, the trainer can easily move forward to slow down forward movement, or move back to galvanize forward or indeed sideways movement. So, if you are standing on the left-hand side of your cob (the usual starting point), with him standing at the wall or fence of the arena ready to work on the left rein, you should stand at his shoulder with your body facing his length. Your left hand holds the left rein close to the bit ring, with your forefinger through the bit ring. The right rein is held in the right hand, which is brought over your cob's neck or withers. The whip is usually held in the right hand along with the right rein. To hold the right rein, I advise doing so with the rein coming out through

This is me in the ideal default position for in-hand work. From this position I can move forward to slow down my cob, I can move back to move her forward or I can step towards her to move her away.

your thumb and forefinger (and then to your cob's mouth) as you can then hold the schooling/dressage whip in the same way with the shaft and lash coming up through your fist from between your thumb and forefinger. (If using a lunge cavesson rather than a snaffle bridle, the hold of the outside rein would be the same, but that of the inside rein would be different in that you would not loop your forefinger into the cavesson ring, but would hold the rein fairly close to it.)

From your starting position, positional changes occur as you signal various movements to your cob and read and respond to his reactions, and all this comes with experience. However, the following exercises and developments will allow you to make informed choices about what to do and how to do it.

LEFT Here I have moved a little forwards of the default position to slow Ketchup down. Note that my whip is pointing down so as not to send mixed messages.

BELOW LEFT Here I am stepping towards Ketchup to move her away from me into a leg-yield step.

BELOW RIGHT Once you are comfortable with the variations of default position you can use a variety of different techniques to bring about a variety of effects. Here I am forward of the default position, slowing Thistle down while driving her quarters sideways with my driving hand and whip to initiate a giravolta.

Basic Changes of Position

Asking for Walk

From the starting position at halt, allow your position to move a little further behind your cob's shoulder (this may be only a slight sway of the body). At the same time, move your eyes away from your cob and towards the direction in which you are going to walk him. This also has the effect of 'opening' your shoulders towards the direction of movement, which provides a subtle cue directing your cob forwards.

Look where you are going.

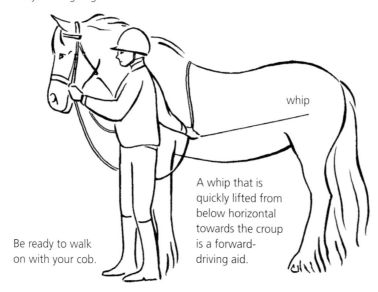

whip

A whip that is quickly lifted from below horizontal towards the croup is a forward-driving aid.

Be ready to walk on with your cob.

How to ask for walk.

At the same time, use the whip in your right hand in an upward direction. This need only be a lift of about 30cm, but can be quite quick with a lethargic cob so as to galvanize forward movement. Expect your cob to walk on and be ready for his first step. Owing to your position beside your cob, as he walks on you will need to step sideways to maintain your in-hand position and keep your frame. Stepping sideways is difficult so be careful! If your cob does not walk on, try again with a little more speed in moving your whip upwards. If this still does not produce the required response, give a little tap of the whip towards his quarters.

Once you achieve the walk, adopt the default position alongside your cob in motion. You'll *feel* the right place as, if you are too far back, your cob will either rush forward or you'll find it harder to maintain control over direction. Remember to praise him as soon as you get the required forward motion.

Halting from Walk

Halting requires repositioning by the handler. As when lungeing, when making a downward transition in-hand, you need to move 'ahead' of your cob. Usually, you do not need to be in front of his head, but

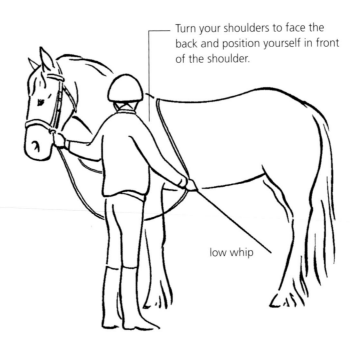

Turn your shoulders to face the back and position yourself in front of the shoulder.

low whip

How to slow and halt a cob in-hand.

moving slightly in front of his shoulder certainly strengthens your body language and helps to 'put the brakes on'. It also helps if you turn your eyes toward your cob's quarters, and turn your shoulder that way too. If these actions have not already brought about the halt, you may wish to move a little more forward while vibrating both reins slightly. At this point it is essential to think about your dominant body language. Think about staying tall, think about pushing your hips forward and staying fairly close to your cob. Be careful with the hand carrying the whip, as you certainly do not want to send mixed messages. Again praise him when you get the halt.

This will be easier once you have worked through flexion exercises and the balancing-the-shoulder exercises (*see* Chapters 2 and 3), as both those exercises with bring about an improvement in your cob's balance and will also give you greater influence over him.

Reading Your Cob

Once you have the ability to move forward as well as halt your cob as described, you also have the ability to regulate speed as required, using increasingly subtle aids of body positioning and language. To slow slightly, move forward in relation to your cob's body, turn your eyes and shoulders slightly towards the rear and vibrate the reins. To move your cob on, move more towards his rear, turn your eyes and shoulders more forward, and use the whip in an upward motion, or give a slight tap.

By using all these variations you will have a fantastic basis for language with your cob; you become the dance partners you hope to be, with you leading and him mirroring your subtle moves.

CHAPTER TWO

In-Hand Flexions

Dispelling Misunderstandings

In-hand flexions are essential exercises on the route towards a light, responsive cob. However, some people are opposed to their use, and this opposition derives partly from their perceived history and partly from a misunderstanding of the philosophy behind their use. Therefore, before discussing how they can be a highly beneficial aid to a cob's in-hand education, it would be helpful to address some misunderstandings.

The historical use of flexions in-hand is largely attributed to the nineteenth-century French riding master François Baucher, a man who achieved remarkable results, but whose methods were controversial in his own time and have remained so ever since. While it is fair to say that his form of flexions is widely viewed as extreme, the flexions I, and others nowadays, advocate are much more moderate. Nonetheless, it is likely that earlier controversy has continued to influence perceptions to this day.

Additionally, there remains opposition to flexions from those who misunderstand the intentions of those who use them in a modern context. Many opponents of flexions say that their use is tantamount to riding the horse 'from front to back' rather than the classically accepted way of riding the horse from his hindquarters into the bridle. It is true that some people do use some systems to 'make a shape' in their horse's neck. These riders are focused only on their horse's head position and neck shape, rather than the whole horse. However, when I make use of flexions, my intention is not to 'make a shape' but rather to 'clear all channels' so that the forehand is ready to receive the energy generated by the quarters. Some types of horse, mainly finer types with a very athletic way of moving, can be ridden 'from behind' without said flexions, the difference being that many of these horses are built 'on the bit' and off the forehand in the first place. With a cob, however, whose balance can so easily be on the forehand, more balance needs to be brought to his body and control brought to the forehand, through moderate and modest flexions of his mouth. This must be achieved before too much energy is put into the system, otherwise that energy will only find its way onto the forehand. However, with the forehand rebalanced through these tiny flexions your cob will easily progress to being 'ridden from behind' without the undoubted pitfall of him collapsing onto his forehand. I must stress here that the changes are mainly small and are in no way 'making a shape'; they are merely a clearing of blockages.

Another argument is that flexions can stop the half-halt effect from influencing the whole horse, working only the horse's head and neck, but my response to this is that the true half-halt is an exercise of the seat and legs far more than of the hands.

Finally some state that flexions will make the horse's neck 'rubbery' but if done with care and without extreme, this will not happen.

Correct Use of Flexions

Correct flexions are tiny exercises whose aiding is made directly down the reins; they affect mainly the mouth, jaw and to some extent the neck of your cob. Most trainers will agree that most resistances occur in the jaw and that those riders who have softness in their horse's mouth generally have suppleness throughout his whole body. Hence the careful use of flexions is essential. In fact, all dressage riders do indeed use small flexions down the rein to maintain softness in contact, rebalance their horses and modify their mount's way of going.

Despite the fact that the flexions described here are moderate in terms of their physical application, their effects are far from moderate – they are the key to softness of contact. There are three main flexions that I use with all of my horses, not just the cobs. While their effects may look small from the onlookers' point of view, the difference in feel is profound and these differences will affect the cob's overall suppleness, balance and posture.

The Flexions I Use

The three flexions I use follow a specific order, as the success of each consecutive flexion is fully dependant on the proficiency and full understanding of that or those that preceded it. The first flexion involves a release of the jaw and allows a drop of the lower jaw, unclenching your cob's teeth and encouraging him to move his tongue gently on the bit, rather like the way you would suck on a hard-boiled sweet. The second flexion gives you lateral control over your cob's mouth, poll and neck. It encourages a slight side-to-side flexion that you could subsequently use in asking for bend or lateral flexion in the lateral movements. The final flexion I use is, in some respects, the least important of the flexions, and one that usually looks after itself if the preceding flexions are fully understood by your cob. It is that of poll flexion. This is the flexion that merely introduces longitudinal flexion, which begins to give your cob the 'on the bit' look. It is, however, only the suggestion of roundness; true roundness comes from the exercises that follow later.

BENEFITS

Many of the benefits have already been discussed. These flexions allow you to ride your cob in true lightness. Many riders come to me with their cobs and complain how heavy they are to ride – heavy in hand and dull off their legs. Through using these flexions, your cob will feel like silk, or melted butter in your hands, light, soft and gentle. This often, in turn, livens up dull individuals, so cobs prepared with these light flexions become forward and active as a consequence. Carrying out these flexions will prepare the muscles in your cob's neck, and even his back, to receive and utilize the energy produced by the hindquarters when this is added.

PREREQUISITES

As these are the starting exercises, the only prerequisite is that your cob is used to being bridled with a simple snaffle, a mullen-mouthed Pelham (with two reins) or, if at a more advanced level, a simple double bridle. If your cob wears a noseband, please make sure it is a simple cavesson and done up loosely enough to allow your cob to truly release his jaw. My bridles very rarely have nosebands as, if done up too tightly, they will limit your cob's ability to release his jaw. Flash, crank and tight cavesson nosebands are a definite no-no. I would recommend drop nosebands for cobs that open their mouths wide or try to get their tongues over the bit. They give sufficient support while still allowing the upper jaw freedom to release.

SEQUENCE OF DEVELOPMENT

1. Release/Mobilization of the Jaw and Softening the Mouth

With your cob standing on the track in the arena, stand at his head with your hand closest to his head holding the inner rein with your forefinger through the snaffle ring (upper ring in a Pelham, or bradoon ring in a double bridle.) The hand closest to your cob's withers should take the other rein and place it half to three-quarters of the way up your cob's neck.

Then, using alternating vibrations, you can 'tickle' your cob's mouth, first with one hand and then with the other. The action should be small and directed slightly upward towards the corner of your cob's mouth rather than backwards, which would put pressure on his tongue.

The response you are looking for in your cob is for him to move his jaw, use his tongue as if moving a boiled sweet in his mouth and lighten the contact. When he does this, stop, release the contact immediately

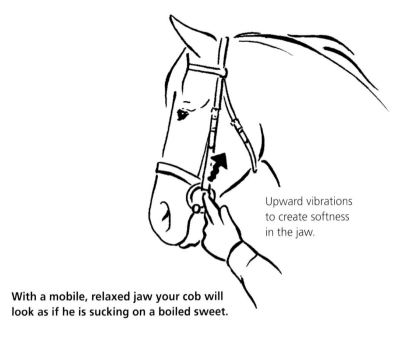

Upward vibrations to create softness in the jaw.

With a mobile, relaxed jaw your cob will look as if he is sucking on a boiled sweet.

and reward him with a pat, a kind word and a titbit. He'll soon realize your intention and be quick to release his jaw for you.

If he does not release his jaw, move the outside rein higher up towards the poll. Vibrate both hands together in a more upward direction. Be quick to see the smallest releases, as the reward given for these small responses will be the route to understanding on your cob's part.

If this still does not achieve the release in the jaw, I would recommend chopping up an apple or carrot to feed to your cob during the exercise; this will show him exactly what you want to achieve and it is far better to do it this way than to increase pressure in the mouth. Remember to stop the exercise and reward even the smallest tendency to release the jaw.

Of course this must be achieved on both reins. Once it can be achieved stationary, you can then ask for a couple of walk steps. As soon as your cob becomes solid, heavy or too still in his jaw or mouth, halt and start again.

2. Lateral Flexion

Once your cob releases his jaw with increasing ease and does so consistently, you are ready to ask for these lateral flexions. This may be after five minutes or after a couple of weeks of the previous activities. The key is to make sure they are truly established first.

In the lateral flexions, you are looking for your cob to maintain the release of the jaw while flexing laterally at the jaw to look slightly to the side with a little flexion throughout the length of the neck.

For these flexions your cob needs to stand at the wall so that he does not try to step out with the hindquarters to escape the action of the flexion.

Once you have softened your cob's jaw using the previous exercise, release the contact on the outside rein while you lift and vibrate the inside rein, asking your cob to look slightly to the inside. You are aiming to turn his head slightly towards you while maintaining the softly moving mouth around the bit. He should not try to push his head down; if he does, return to the earlier exercise to re-establish softness and rudimentary self-carriage. Similarly, if he becomes heavy in your hand or stops moving his mouth around the bit, go back to the mobilization activities above.

Once you can achieve the desired result with flexions to the inside, try the exercise to the outside. Instead of relaxing the outside contact, maintain the vibration on the rein that comes over your cob's neck. As you increase the vibration and upward action on the outside rein, relax your inside rein and allow it to push out slightly as your cob flexes to the outside.

As before, once this is easily achieved stationary, take it for a walk. Maintain it for a step or two and then reward. Again, if the qualities of lightness and softness disappear, you should halt and re-establish. As always, this needs to be achieved on both reins.

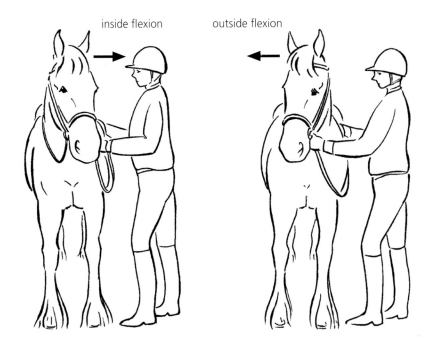

inside flexion   outside flexion

Showing inside flexion and outside flexion.

3. Flexion at the Poll, Rounding the Neck

Once your cob maintains a softly mouthing contact with the bit, without pushing down onto the bit, and can maintain this while flexing in both directions, then the final mini-flexion should be easily achieved and will only be necessary if your cob has not already adopted a more rounded frame.

Ask your cob to give you more lateral flexion to the inside – this time maintain a slight vibration on the outside rein too. Your cob should give you an inside flexion while offering a more rounded neck, and a slight nod of the head so that his profile comes closer to the vertical position (closer, but not yet vertical). As soon as he gives you a little poll flexion, stop and reward.

His poll should stay high, but if he drops his poll low go back to the first flexion exercise to soften his mouth, raise his poll and re-establish that all-important first element of self-carriage. (Self-carriage starts here and will be much more basic than the self-carriage expected at a higher level.)

Again, this needs to become established on the move. Once the earlier flexions are established, then I find this step more or less takes care of itself.

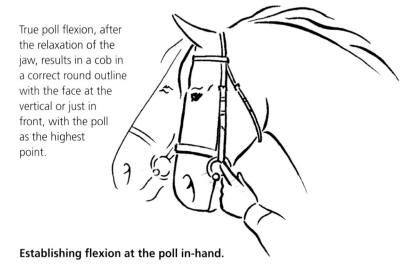

True poll flexion, after the relaxation of the jaw, results in a cob in a correct round outline with the face at the vertical or just in front, with the poll as the highest point.

Establishing flexion at the poll in-hand.

CHAPTER THREE

In-Hand Shoulder Balance

This is very much a necessary part of your cob's education. Cobs are renowned for being 'on the shoulder', for falling in, falling out and for powering on through the shoulder like bulldozers. Once the flexions and lightness are in place, we need to develop balance a little further back so that, when ridden later on, the power from the hindquarters does not just plop the weight onto the forehand. This is

Here I am controlling Ketchup's balance off her right shoulder. This is the preliminary exercise that precedes all others.

necessary for developing bend and balance on circles as well as self-carriage and ease of movement in lateral work.

What is Shoulder Balance?

Shoulder balance is a posture adopted by your cob once he has learned to be soft in the contact and to give a more advanced level of bend, in which he can begin to use his inside hind leg to prop up his balance and remove some of the weight off his inside shoulder. It is basically that intermediate step between 'going straight' and 'going sideways'. It shows your cob how to be responsible for his own shoulder balance and that, when bent into any particular direction, his body does not need to follow his nose. With many cobs this is indeed key and can be one thing that stops your cob from being the stereotypical 'tank of a cob'.

BENEFITS

The benefits are multi-dimensional and affect all areas of your cob's ridden career. For a start, it is the next step on from flexing and softening your cob's contact. It often means that your cob will adopt a more sophisticated posture of bend and outline and will give you, as his rider and trainer, more control by which to mould and sculpt his body in a more subtle way. As mentioned earlier, it is also one more step in preparing your cob to accept the forward impulsion necessary to be ridden from the hind end, and will mean that the energy produced later by the hindquarters will be able to follow a seamless channel to your cob's mouth, rather than plonking him onto his shoulders. His rhythm will be vastly improved as the balance will not be dragged down onto his forehand, and his back will be less solid. Therefore, by carrying out this preparatory work, you will have hopefully ironed out many of the creases and be ready for the proper work.

PREREQUISITES

You must have control over your own and your cob's direction and speed when working in-hand. I always advise people to arrange a circle of cones in the arena. Using the cones gives you something to aim for and effectively gives you, the trainer, control over direction. Then, once you are walking cone to cone with your cob, I recommend that you alter speed. Slow down, and expect your cob to slow down too. Keep your body language dominant and strong, stay erect and keep your pelvis pushed forward, and keep in mind that he needs to accommodate you in terms of speed. Then speed up again and expect your cob to move along faster. Use your forward aid with your whip if need be. Repeat until these exercises are easy for both of you.

Your cob must also be able to give slightly in his mouth and give a little inside flexion to really achieve this. This balancing work must not be attempted until these criteria are established otherwise you'll get yourself into some kind of wrestling match with your cob. As strength plays no part in training horses, this is not the way forward and would be the most likely way for your cob to realize his own strength, with negative consequences.

SEQUENCE OF DEVELOPMENT

Once your prerequisites are in place and you are ready to start this work, I would recommend you start on the wall of your arena, with you positioned on the outside. This stops any claustrophobic tendencies with your cob becoming anxious and also helps with a cob that adopts speed as an escape. So, once positioned on the outside of your cob (positioned on his left on the right rein), take the left rein and bit ring in your left hand and take the right rein over his neck about three-quarters of the way down towards his withers. Your right hand, holding the rein and whip, will be positioned just above the point of the shoulder at the lower edge of his neck. This is where your right hand needs to palpate to soften the balance of the shoulder. Palpate, pulse, vibrate but certainly not push! Pushing would only show you how much your cob would push back into pressure. Making sure that the pressure is 'on and off' ensures that your aids are not just 'on' all the time, gives your cob time to respond and ultimately allows your cob to approach a suitable self-carriage at this level.

Initially all this is done at the halt but it should not take too long, and it is used mainly to let you, the trainer, get accustomed to the aiding, as being stationary is not the ideal starting point from which to lighten the shoulders. Once you are comfortable, move on to walk.

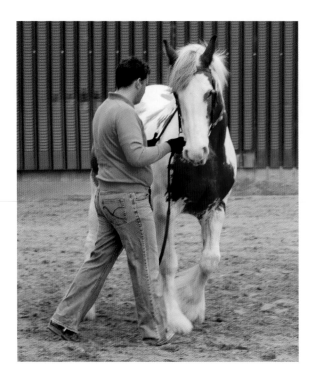

Here Ketchup and I are on an inner track with me closest to the wall (on the outside, wall out of view). I am preparing for a leg-yield and, to start, I am asking Ketchup for the balance off the shoulder.

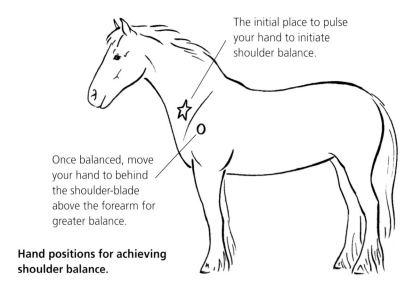

The initial place to pulse your hand to initiate shoulder balance.

Once balanced, move your hand to behind the shoulder-blade above the forearm for greater balance.

Hand positions for achieving shoulder balance.

First, make sure the walk steps are fairly slow but impulsive. Ask for the softness in the mouth using both reins, then ask for left flexion with your left hand and then, when all feels right, begin to pulse on your cob's 'sweet spot' above the point of his shoulder where his brachio-cephalic muscle appears to meet his shoulder- blade. The magical feeling (and you'll know as soon as your cob offers it) is an instant lightness in his mouth, and instant lightness in his shoulders and an increase in bend.

You may find that your cob gives you *too much* bend and runs away from the pressure in a more exaggerated way. In this case, move your right hand further back, allowing the reins to cross over at the withers or even further back and, rather than pulsing on your cob's side, allow your hand to vibrate the rein and look for the softness in your hands again.

As always, this work needs to be done on both reins. You will no doubt find that, on one rein, your cob runs a little sideways, in which case you'll need to use a little more outside rein to control it, while on the other rein your cob is likely to find it harder to give you that balance. All we are looking for initially is one step in balance. Once achieved, stop and reward your cob. He'll enjoy the reward and it will make him want to offer his response to you more promptly and for longer. He'll enjoy pleasing you as much as he'll enjoy his rewards.

Next, you'll be able to adopt the position to the inside of your cob, with him directly next to the wall. The sequence is identical to that just described; the greater complexity comes from your position on the inside, which gives you less strength and control over speed, as well as making some cobs feel the anxiety associated with claustrophobia. Make sure you do not get too close to your cob and end up pushing him to the wall. If need be, think about working on an inner track a little off the wall. This will give your cob room to push his inside shoulder out towards the wall a little without getting too close to it. It is often at this point that trainers lose some control because they get so engrossed in the cob's shoulder, they forget to control speed and direction. To help with this I would urge you to keep your eyes looking into the direction in which you are going, and to keep your legs going at the same speed independently of your hands. Looking into the direction you are walking keeps you in control, and keeps you aware of how fast you are going and where you are in the arena. This awareness over speed, direction and position ensures that you can work your hands for flexion and shoulder balance without them affecting the speed you are going. This will also ensure that, as you ask for flexion and for your cob to lighten his shoulder, you will not be conned into getting faster and faster, a way for your cob to escape the gymnastic effect of the exercise.

Once you can do this, it is time to get your cones out again and take the balance off your cob's inside shoulder on a circle line. Again, all of the advice given so far is still relevant in this exercise. Your eyes must keep looking where you are going so that you can maintain control over direction. You must be in control of your cob's speed, even when you bring your hands into work for flexions and balance of the shoulders. This is the preliminary exercise to the giravolta (*see* Chapter 5), the highly gymnastic, suppling exercise so characteristic of many classical schools.

CHAPTER FOUR

In-Hand Transitions

Transitions from Halt to Walk and Back

So far we have progressed sufficiently to work through a sequence of transitions from halt to walk and back. In schooling it is the use of transitions that begins to build towards collection in your cob. I often think that each transition, or set of transitions, 'blow ups' a balloon of stored energy, which manifests itself by a cob getting lighter and

Asking Thistle to walk on. A lifting driving aid from the whip as I am about to turn my shoulders and walk with her.

more responsive without being 'sharp'. He begins to develop a pelvic tilt which brings his back up, and concertinas his hind legs, making him 'sit' somewhat more on his hocks, and his steps become much more cat-like.

To develop this further I advise continuing to work your cob through repeated and frequent transitions from halt to walk and back. At first you would not necessarily count the walk steps (by which I mean steps of the forelegs, not complete strides) but, over time, you should expect your cob to become more precise with this work. When your cob halts with easy aids, and does not push into your hands or try to speed up in the walk, then you are ready to proceed to more complex sequences. First of all, I would suggest ten walk steps, halt, ten walk steps, halt. Once you are comfortable with this, reduce to eight steps, then five. Quite quickly you'll notice that your cob really pays attention to your body language – he'll want to mirror your actions as much as possible, especially if you have been lavish with your praise.

Developing the Trot

Once your cob is developing his transitions between halt and walk, it will be time to introduce shortened strides of trot. Using a gait with more forward energy than walk will automatically result in more stored energy as well. Since your cob is expending more energy for the forward motion, his willingness and expectation to do so mean that a higher level of energy is at your disposal. This energy will be available to develop increased collection when the cob is engaged in the repeated transition exercises. This is, however, dependant on all the prerequisites for lightness, inside flexion and balance of the inside shoulder being maintained throughout the trot work.

Before you can use trot within any repeated transition exercises under saddle, you need to establish it in basic in-hand work.

From the walk on the left rein, with you on the left-hand side of your cob, establish slight inside flexion; make sure your cob is slightly round in outline, but keep his poll high. Then begin to increase the speed of your walk. At the same time, use your whip in an upward direction to help drive your cob a little more forward. Once he has given you a diagonalized step or two of trot (jog even!), stop and praise him for his efforts. During these trot steps remember to go forward with your cob, especially in these early stages, as you do not want to give him mixed messages.

Repeat these upward transitions until he pops into the trot easily, begins to read your body language and responds more and more to your quickening steps. At this point you can stop jogging on; quickening your walk will be enough. At this stage it will become more and more important to keep the soft inside flexion through the trot work. Ask for the trot, and keep a vibration on the left rein as your cob steps forward into trot. If your cob finds it difficult to repeat the transitions to trot with a little more flexion on the inside rein, you may need to reinforce this in the halt to walk transitions. Once you are more comfortable about your influence over your cob's flexion in the halt to walk transition, you should not have too much difficulty when you return to the walk to trot and back to walk transitions. When he gives you what you want, even briefly, praise him so he knows he's on the right track.

Once he can do this, ask for a little more balance off the inside shoulder as you did in the walk. Again, praise as soon as this is achieved. Try then to pick up walk before things disintegrate. The aids to walk from trot are the same as the aids to halt from walk, or indeed from trot as well. Feel a little more in front of your cob, slow your movement and remember to keep your hips pushed forward and remain solid in your own position.

Of course, all of these exercises must be done on both reins.

Developing the Rein-Back

The last of the movements used with these transition exercises is the rein-back. It really is the key to the supreme pelvic tilt, flexion of the haunches and the concertina effect of the hind leg joint system, all of which are an absolute necessity for true collection to develop. Rein-back is often started quite early in a young horse's education as he learns to move away from the direction of the handler, and the cob is no different. Quite often, a well-handled cob will have been taught to move back in the stable by his handler, and this lesson may have been further developed in his leading education, for example when manoeuvring around gates at turnout time. However, once the preceding exercises have been perfected, now comes the time to formalize your cob's education in the rein-back.

Here Ketchup is just about to step into the rein-back prior to the piaffe. It is with these transitions that the work towards piaffe begins.

Part of the rein-back aid derives from your body positioning. So, from your usual in-hand position on the left-hand side of your cob, with him positioned on the left rein, move a little more forward in front of your cob's shoulder. Turn your shoulders to face more backwards, thereby using your body as a barrier to direct your cob's movement in a backward motion. From this position, with your cob in halt, place your right hand (which is also carrying the whip) on the point of his shoulder. Pulse a little with your right hand and make sure you avoid any steady pressure, which would make your cob push back at you. At the same time as pulsing your hand, say the word 'back' in an assertive voice; expect him to ease his weight back and take a step to the rear. When he does, be quick to cease the aids and reward him.

If he does not take a step backwards, increase the pressure applied, but still by pulsing. If this still does not work, move your hand into the soft tissue directly below where the cob's windpipe disappears into the torso. Pulse here with your fingertips and increase the pressure of the pulse until he takes a step. By moving your fingers to this soft tissue you are making things slightly more uncomfortable for him and, of course, it is absolutely necessary that as soon as he responds, you release the pressure and praise. Then you can put your pulsing hand back on the point of his shoulder and ask with your hand there.

Once he can step back consistently like this, it is time to ask for more steps. Starting from one step, proceed to three, four and then five steps, or (just a few) more. Make sure you can control the number of steps; if he tries to 'take over' the rein-back steps you need to ask him to step forwards, using the whip in the normal way.

You are looking for your cob to move back more and more from the voice rather than from too much pressure, so matching your verbal aid to every hand aid will help for the future.

When you can ask your cob to step back in this way it is time to ask him to stay in a rounded outline and maintain the contact. So, from your normal in-hand position, ask for roundness and softness to the inside so he does not step back too crookedly. (Make sure that this softness is true relaxation of the jaw, and that your cob has not just twisted his neck to the inside in order to soften to your aids. If he twists his neck to the inside, the balance will not be great and indeed straightness will not be maintained.) Then, use your voice command, 'back', so he knows what is required of him.

In all schooling, forward impulse is essential. This is so even in the rein-back, where the 'forwardness' is being redirected into the steps backwards. To achieve this 'forward energy' in the rein-back you can start to position your whip horizontally towards your cob's hindquarters and hip. This should be sufficient to generate that forward energy, which is then redirected by your secure body positioning and your rein-back aiding, which includes your voice. What you must avoid, however, is over-aiding with the whip, which could make your cob rush forwards, and push against you. (Alternatively, it could even make your cob rush backwards as an overreaction. Moderate, gentle aiding and direction from the whip is the key. Forward impulse is better built up over time, as this will avoid over-aiding, confusion and loss of balance and harmony.

Again ask for one step initially and then, when your cob's confidence in the exercise improves, you can ask for more steps back.

Complex Transitions

Now you can work in-hand in walk, trot and rein-back, you have a basis for developing full impulsion, sitting your cob fully onto his haunches and seeking absolute lightness of contact, and working towards the lightness of the shoulders that epitomizes correct dressage. You now have the tools in your kit to develop some of the most advanced dressage movements, such as the expression of ultimate collection: the piaffe.

Training Considerations

To work towards these qualities you now need to develop a repertoire of transition work that enhances your cob's qualities as well as developing his weaknesses. Generally speaking, your cob will either tend to be hot and fast in his transitions, or he will be slow and lazy, and you need to respond appropriately and consider using these exercises to modify these extremes. However, the exercises and their sequences are identical – it is the trainer's focus that needs to change, depending on the cob's natural way of working.

It may be that you will work with the intention of slowing and calming your cob if he is 'sharp'; conversely you may need to work in an energizing and motivating way if your cob is lazy. If your cob is 'sharp', take more time and ask slowly, calmly and keep your own energy low. If your cob is lazy, expect him to react quickly, and be more demanding; feel full of energy yourself and do not be afraid to make more upward transitions.

Sequences such as walk to rein-back to walk, walk to rein-back to trot, trot to walk to trot and rein-back to trot will really help to develop impulsion. Remember to change the sequences regularly and work on both reins, so that your cob does not anticipate and take over the exercises.

CHAPTER FIVE

The Giravolta

One of the earliest steps in the cob's education is to develop the giravolta, a classical exercise much used by trainers in Spain and Portugal. Through the development of this most gymnastic exercise, the language of equitation is established between horse and rider. It is the very start of the thread that will be woven into all other movements, and develops the skills necessary for both cob and trainer to make further progress.

What is the Giravolta?

The giravolta is a highly gymnastic exercise related to leg-yielding (*see* Chapter 6), which can bring great benefits performed in-hand. In the giravolta, the cob maintains bend and flexion to the inside while his body steps out and away from the created bend. The introductory

The advanced form of giravolta.

form of this exercise requires mild bend, and only a small amount of lateral crossing of the cob's legs, as cob and trainer describe a circle of 10–15m. While cob and trainer walk around the circle line, the cob, showing soft flexion to the inside, should begin to step out of the circle line with his hind legs. The flexion and bend should not be extreme, but the cob should maintain a steady rhythm and begin to show signs of increased suppleness.

The moderate form of the exercise describes a smaller circle of 5–8m and the cob is required to show greater bend, and more crossing of legs, as well as a more sophisticated and supple way of going, with improved self-carriage. In this more advanced exercise, the cob will need to show increased lateral crossing of both his fore and hind legs. The rhythm is maintained and amplified, with more deliberate stepping and a greater degree of collection and articulation of the cob's hind leg joint system and a higher, more accentuated stepping of the forelegs.

BENEFITS

The benefits of the development of this exercise are numerous – the giravolta truly is indispensable in training healthy, supple horses, including cobs. The development of this exercise gives the trainer the ability to control every part of the cob's body. It teaches the cob to yield to pressure and move away from sideways-driving aids. The exercise itself supples the cob both laterally and longitudinally, it develops controlled bend and the adduction/abduction of the cob's limbs. It is particularly proficient at suppling cobs in their loins, especially at the point where the longissimus dorsi muscle meets the gluteals – a point that, in many riding horses, is often in a state of stress and tension. The giravolta improves the cob's ability to collect and develops the all-important pelvic tuck that is so necessary for future exercises. For all of these reasons, it is not uncommon to see horses on the Iberian Peninsula being warmed up using this technique for up to half an hour at a time.

PREREQUISITES

In essence, the giravolta will be the test of the quality of the work done so far. If resistance is shown through the development of the giravolta, you can be sure that the mistake will be found somewhere in the earlier training of the 'in-hand essentials'. As such, its remedy must be found in earlier training, in much the same way as unravelling a patch of knitting to find the dropped stitch earlier in the work. The giravolta basically brings together all facets of the essential training and melds them into one progressive exercise, upon which all future lateral work will be based.

In the initial stages of the giravolta, the trainer will need to ensure a positive use of posture and positioning that will bring about a re-positioning of posture in the cob as well as being used by the cob as a source of balance. The cob must show certain 'submission' to the flexions by maintaining a soft and mobile mouth, a rounded outline, and inside flexion and bend, without losing balance through the carefully positioned shoulders.

It sounds as though there are a lot of prerequisites, but only by practising the giravolta will you know if the quality of the early basic training has been of a high enough standard. Being the first exercise that brings together all areas of education thus far, it provides opportunities to work the cob through a specific exercise while, at the same time, highlighting areas of earlier training that need improvement. This testing, as it were, of earlier work also illustrates one truth I always strive to impart – that if you only school on 20m circles you will only ever get 20m circles! To advance, you need to make a leap of faith as well as a leap of schooling.

SEQUENCE OF DEVELOPMENT

Control of the Shoulders

From the earlier exercise of walking round a circle of about 15m diameter while balancing flexion to the inside with a slight rebalancing of the inside shoulder to the outside, you can begin to exert greater and greater control of the shoulders. Softness of the cob's mouth as well as slight inside flexion must be maintained at all times. If either of these essentials is missing, abort the attempt and re-establish the missing quality. To help, in the initial stages, it might be worth slowing everything down to give your cob, as well as yourself, time to work out how to maintain the essentials while adding the new balance, with the cob's shoulders a little more to the outside.

Here I am preparing for a giravolta and I'm asking Ketchup to control her shoulders in readiness for the difficult movement.

So, from your default position (say on the left rein), once the circle line and the qualities of flexion in the mouth and neck are established, begin to ask your cob to balance his shoulders a little more to the outside. Do this by using your right hand positioned about halfway down his shoulder. As the cob's shoulder swings back, just before the left foreleg picks up, begin to vibrate or pulse your right hand on your cob's shoulder. Do not just try to push your cob over, as sustained pressure is always pressed into, and the cob will give you the direct opposite of what you require by pushing his shoulder towards you. Your left hand, holding on to the rein or bit ring, vibrates gently to maintain a mobile, soft mouth, and slight flexion towards you. If your cob does not seem to want to move his shoulder over, increase the intensity of the pulse but remember, *just a pulse*, otherwise your cobby friend will only push back at you. If he walks too fast, or loses the softness in his mouth or the neck flexion to the inside, stop the exercise and re-establish your basics. As your cob begins to move his left foreleg out over towards his right foreleg, allow him to balance as much as he can on his own. The moment he has given you a second of moving away from your pulses, stop and reward him. Soon, he will understand what you want and smaller and smaller pulses and vibrations will achieve the same balance.

Owing to natural crookedness and one-sidedness you will find your cob more reluctant on one rein and fairly enthusiastic on the other, depending on which is his naturally concave side. This will, of course, be a common theme throughout your cob's schooling and will be seen in many exercises. It is through working on these exercises that this crookedness will be straightened, and the so-called one-sidedness will even out. If your cob moves easily off the inside shoulder but you feel he is moving *too much* to the outside, stop pulsing with your right hand and, holding the outside rein over his shoulder, ask your cob to straighten and to slow down. Take slower steps yourself and wait for your cob to accommodate your slower movement.

As ever, this must be practised on both reins; on one rein making sure your cob moves easily off the pressure on his shoulder, and on the other making sure he does not bend too much at the withers and purely thrust out through his shoulder in a typical jack-knifing position.

Once your cob is moving easily on both reins, you can move on to the basic stage of the giravolta. Often this will happen within the first or second in-hand schooling session after your cob has offered the essentials successfully.

Basic Early Giravolta

Once your cob can balance off the inside shoulder, while maintaining softness in his mouth and a certain roundness in his neck, you can begin to work a little more 'true bend' into his way of going. Again

Here I am using my hand on Ketchup's shoulder to maintain shoulder balance while my whip moves her quarters away and out onto a large giravolta.

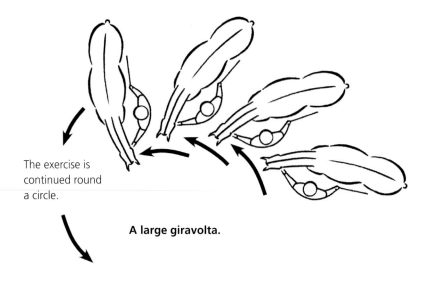

The exercise is
continued round
a circle.

A large giravolta.

on the left rein (for clarity), once your cob is stepping lightly away from your softer vibrations on his shoulder, you can slip your hand slightly behind his shoulder to just in front of the girth area. Your aiding remains the same as before; slight pulsing or vibrating of your hand with plenty of releases of pressure to ensure 'self-carriage'. What you are looking for now is for your cob to maintain his balance off his inside shoulder while giving a little more bend and side-stepping away from the pressure in the new part of his body. You will probably find that he will lose his balance a few times before he 'cracks it'. Each time he loses his balance, stop and re-establish first the essentials, followed by the balance off his inside shoulder, before moving your hand again. Only ask for one step and, once you get it, stop and praise him as this is how he knows he is doing what you want of him. The process, for the time being, is exactly the same as for the earlier exercise of controlling your cob's shoulders.

Eventually, as you glance back at your cob's hind legs, you will see that they are displacing to the outside of the circle. At this stage, of course, it will not be a huge amount – maybe the equivalent of a shoulder-fore where the inside hind leg steps forwards to midway between the lines created by both of his forelegs. Once he can do this easily (and this is often in the first session practising this new dance, but please do wait until that ease is not only evident but also consistent), you can begin to move your right hand a little further back to where your leg would rest if you were practising this exercise ridden. Again, the actual aiding is the same as before, but the hand position must be assumed after the shoulder balance and the initial slight angle are established. It is too much to expect of an inexperienced cob for your hand to go straight to the girth area where your leg would rest, and have him understand and react correctly. Take things step by step. However, once it is a practicality to place your hand in position just behind the girth area, where your leg would hang, you are looking for your cob to take deliberate, measured steps to the outside of the circle in an angle equivalent to a three-track version of shoulder-in. At this stage you are not looking for your cob to step out any more than on the three track lines around your 15m circle. Expecting more at this stage would undoubtedly unbalance your cob, putting him on his forehand and losing control as his momentum carries him sideways, rather than being an effective use of his musculature.

At this point you should notice that your steps will slow down as your cob gains more bend and develops rudimentary engagement in his hindquarters. This will be evidence of your cob beginning to use his body in a different way. He should begin to articulate his joints, especially those in his hind legs and, rather than 'covering ground', the steps become higher and slightly more stylized. This through schooling will, in due course, be harnessed and developed into true collection. Again, this exercise must be practised on both reins.

Moderate Giravolta (Working Giravolta)

Why the term 'working giravolta'? Because this is the part of the exercise that is the foundation for collection and self-carriage, as well as all the classical lateral movements described later. However, this is where the giravolta can become a little complicated and it is where most mistakes are made. This usually happens because trainers become so engrossed in the crossing of their cob's hind legs that they neglect the essentials and forget to maintain that delicate balance of their cob's shoulders. For this form of giravolta, two different things need to happen, and they need to happen simultaneously. The size of the giravolta circle needs to be almost halved from about 15m to about 8m and, while making the circle smaller, you need to begin to ask your cob for more lateral crossing of the hind legs out away from the pulsing of your hand.

The overall sequence of events here follows that previously described – the balancing of the shoulders and the development of a little more

CLOCKWISE FROM TOP LEFT
This sequence shows three moments of a small giravolta. The focus here is on sufficient crossing of the legs behind, while maintaining shoulder balance and lightness in the mouth.

bend and a little more crossing on the larger circle. Once you have established this, you will need to slow your walking down further, feeling as though you are wrapping your cob's whole forehand around you, while maintaining that balance off the inside shoulder. When you start walking more slowly, reduce the size of the circle while pulsing for increased side-stepping of the hind legs. I often imagine a force-field between me and any cob I work with at this stage. This image helps maintain that balance off the inside shoulder, while bringing the whole forehand around me as a balancing pole, increasing bend and creating a more sophisticated balance. This is usually the point at which the trainer feels a change in balance in the cob – it is where self-carriage during in-hand work is first felt! The moment you feel a little more side-stepping from the cob's hind legs, while maintaining balance off that inside shoulder, stop and praise your cob. He has just made the first step to improved balance, even if you have not quite got down to an 8m size of circle.

You can often get to this point in a cob's in-hand education fairly rapidly, perhaps within a week or two of starting in-hand work. But this is where it is necessary to be careful, as pushing beyond this point when your cob is not ready can make him lose confidence, or even overstretch his delicate loins.

At this point in the work, you can begin to develop the leg-yielding and other lateral exercises described in the following chapters, before continuing towards the advanced stages of the giravolta. What has been developed so far is sufficient as a basis for the shoulder-in, renvers, travers and half-pass. You can only progress to the advanced form of giravolta once these lateral exercises have been developed.

....

CHAPTER SIX

In-Hand Leg-Yielding

I find it very surprising how so many people consider this movement to be 'quite advanced' when in fact I use it very early on in any horse's education. Without the effects and control established by introducing leg-yielding, the rider does not necessarily have the tools to establish true bend, to ride 'from the inside leg to the outside rein', or purely the ability to place the cob where required. As I've mentioned, many cobs are renowned for being 'on the shoulder', for falling in, falling out and for powering along like bulldozers. However, once a cob can under-stand that the leg does not just mean 'faster', but can, in fact, mean 'move over' or 'engage', the tug of war between cob and rider ends and true riding in lightness begins. Leg-yielding is the preliminary lateral movement, often introduced before the shoulder-in, and though it's a very easy exercise it is one that can move a cob and his rider on in terms of schooling levels, balance and control. It is the earliest move-ment that allows riding and schooling to take on a more sophisticated, mature form.

What is Leg-Yielding?

Leg-yielding is the simplest of the lateral movements in that there is no collection required. In the ridden form, the cob steps forward and sideways in a diagonal movement away from the pressure of the rider's leg. In the case of in-hand work, the movement is away from the pulsing pressure of the trainer's hand, which acts as a substitute for the rider's

Ketchup showing the classic engaging steps of leg-yield. Her bend and flexion are to the left, while she is crossing her legs and travelling to the right.

leg. The cob keeps a little inside bend and steps out away from the bend. Most trainers think of leg-yielding as a movement that is performed with a virtually straight horse, with only slight flexion at the poll. I, however, perform it with a little more bend through the whole of the cob's body, and think of it much more as an intermediate step between the giravolta and the shoulder-in, in that the amount of bend is closer to that of the shoulder-in but without the same level of engagement, and therefore the exercise is a stepping stone towards this more sophisticated movement. Executed in this way I believe it has its true place in classical equitation, where its development contributes to the whole of the cob's education rather than being a stand-alone exercise, which is not necessarily developed from any other classical exercise and does not contribute to any that are to follow. If it is thought of as an intermediate step between these movements, one can understand its development and its place in the training of future exercises such as shoulder-in and travers.

BENEFITS

Once the leg-yield is developed in-hand, you really are starting to work more and more of your cob's muscles, readying them for more complex and demanding exercises. Both the abductor and adductor muscles of the limbs will start to be conditioned. Leg-yielding begins to give your cob the benefits of true suppleness, evidenced by his ability to bend and to maintain that bend while stepping sideways. It contributes to the development of strength in the hind limbs by virtue of the fact that one hind leg pushes harder than the other (a very clear reason why, as ever, this exercise must be practised on both reins to ensure even development) and it enhances acceptance of the contact by maintaining softness to the inside while the hind leg on the same side drives under and across the cob's body. Therefore, although leg-yielding is not a collected movement, it begins to condition your cob's muscular system and prepares him for the more controlled work of collection.

PREREQUISITES

If you have followed the order of exercises explained so far, you and your cob will be ready to start developing leg-yielding. Of course, each of the previously discussed qualities is essential but lightness in contact is a must for every step. Once lightness is lost, the exercise must be stopped and lightness re-established. We want our cob to be light and responsive, and to carry on regardless would be the way to turn him into the heavy bulldozer that any cob has the potential to be. This we must avoid at all costs. So you must be able to maintain that lightness in the contact, with a slight inside flexion, balancing off the inside shoulder. Being able to step laterally around a circle with ease, while maintaining these qualities, lets you know he is ready for this next stage.

SEQUENCE OF DEVELOPMENT

Once your giravolta work is being performed with ease on both reins, you can take your giravolta circle from the middle of the arena towards one of the corners. Once into the corner, make a sweep of giravolta steps, which will bring you out onto the inner track, and from there take a few steps straight out towards the track. As you do this, maintain inside flexion and begin to ask your cob's whole body to step out (I would stress whole body here, rather than just his quarters). To achieve this, I find it helpful to bring my driving hand more forward again toward the cob's shoulder (the driving hand on the left rein would be the right hand). By using the inner track, you are only asking for two steps of leg-yield out of the giravolta.

If your cob wants to swing his quarters over too much, you may need to move your driving hand more forward again and work in a similar way to balancing his shoulders, as described in Chapter 3. Maintain inside flexion while your driving hand pulses just behind the shoulder. This should correct any quarters-first tendencies.

If your cob gives you too much neck bend and rushes sideways through the shoulder, ask for less inside flexion and think about stepping forward more, only thinking about a half-step sideways at a time before stepping forwards again. Using more of the outside rein, which is coming over your cob's withers to your driving hand, in a vibrating manner, should stop him pushing his shoulders out.

Once you can leg-yield from the giravolta on the inner track back to the track, it is time to increase the distance you are requiring from your cob in his leg-yield. Aim to straighten your giravolta onto the three-quarter line and leg-yield back out to the track. From there, you can move your giravoltas over more towards the centre line and leg-yield out to the track. Again, watch that your cob moves over at your speed. If he tries to take over, return to stepping more forward and only ask for half a step of leg-yield at a time. If lightness is lost, stop and take a step back and re-establish it, along with correct flexion and balance, before trying again.

Now you can try leg-yielding without the giravolta to set things up. Try turning down the three-quarter line (and later the centre line)

ABOVE LEFT Ketchup is taking her last step of the giravolta. I am preparing to move Ketchup diagonally into a leg-yield.

ABOVE RIGHT And now I have moved my shoulders, thereby moving all of Ketchup's body sideways away from me. Notice the driving whip.

Here, from a turn onto the centre line, we are taking our first step into a leg-yield.

Next step. Here Ketchup shows how flexible she actually is at stretching out sideways …

… and here how easily she can step across.

and leg-yielding out to the track. When you first attempt this, it may take your cob longer to start moving sideways than previously. Do not worry too much about that but, for the first couple of attempts, the moment he steps sideways let him know how pleased you are with him. As soon as he knows what is expected of him he'll move over easily and immediately.

Once you can make a turn and leg-yield without the giravolta you can pick up the shortened trot that you have been developing and try leg-yielding from that. Again, start from an inner track and gradually make the gap bigger by starting on the three-quarter line and then the centre line. If it goes wrong, do not panic; return to walk and re-establish all your prerequisites. Take it slowly, be mindful, and you should find your progress will be swift!

You are now well on your way to having a real 'ballroom partner' who can begin to manoeuvre through increasingly difficult routines, the choreography of which is only limited by imagination. Now you are ready to build in all of your transitions incorporating walk, trot, halt and rein-back. Not only will your work together be increasingly

Once proficient in the exercise, body language becomes the dominant aid. Here Ketchup watches me carefully and mirrors me beautifully.

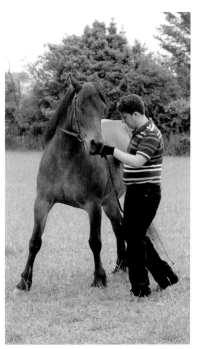

Thistle is trying hard to mirror my body but has tried just a little too hard and has fallen out through her shoulder. Encouraging slow steps will help.

Better balance, outline and steps.

beautiful, but it is truly becoming bodywork for your cob of a very real kind, in the way Pilates or gymnastics are for humans. He should start to look great, supple and full of presence after his in-hand schooling session. His posture should be improving and he should be maturing mentally, whatever his age, old or young.

....

CHAPTER SEVEN

In-Hand Shoulder-In and Counter Shoulder-In

These are the first truly collecting movements that we will begin to school. Along with the use of the transitions already mentioned, plus the rein-back, the shoulder-in and the counter shoulder-in will further develop the tilt of your cob's pelvis, which will be the basis for all work to come and will really develop his topline muscles as well as strengthening his core muscles. Through performing the shoulder-in and its mirror opposite movement the counter shoulder-in, not only will your cob be able to synchronize his movements with yours, mirroring your body language with his own, but he will develop that suppleness necessary to wrap his body around yours (and later around your leg under saddle), giving a more sophisticated bend as he uses this graceful suppleness to glide from one movement to another. Imagine your cob being able to change bend like liquid butter, sliding softly from bend to bend. Imagine him being so supple in his bend that he can hold his own bend, in true self-carriage.

What are Shoulder-In and Counter Shoulder-In?

Shoulder-In

Shoulder-in is a lateral movement in which your cob will be bent to the inside, while his shoulders, too, are brought to the inside and he is moving laterally out away from the bend. So in shoulder-in to the right,

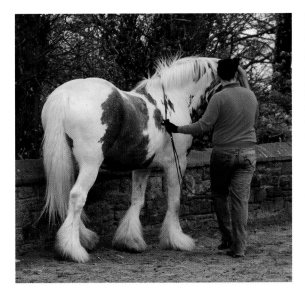 

your cob would be bent to the right, his shoulders brought in to the right, but he will be stepping forward towards his left shoulder. When viewed from the front (in the form of shoulder-in commonly seen in competition) your cob should be on three tracks, described as follows: the hind leg closest to the wall is on a track of its own; the outside foreleg is brought in and is on the same track as the inside hind leg; the inside foreleg is on a track of its own, towards the inside of the arena. The mean angle of the cob's body is often described as being thirty degrees in from the track if viewed from above. Some argue that shoulder-in can and should be performed on four tracks at a greater angle than that described. I have no problem with this as long as the increased angle is achieved as a result of greater bend as opposed to the hind legs stepping out and escaping the collecting influence of the movement. If you aim for the four-track shoulder-in, practise the three-track movement as a preliminary exercise; only when this is of a good standard should you try to increase the bend to produce a more advanced shoulder-in on four tracks.

ABOVE LEFT The shoulder-in shown in-hand. The near hind is on a track of its own. The off hind and near fore are on the same track by virtue of the shoulders being brought to the right. The off fore is brought to an inner track in its own tracking.

ABOVE RIGHT The counter shoulder-in, the sister movement and mirror image of shoulder-in.

Counter Shoulder-In

Counter shoulder-in is an identical movement to shoulder-in in all aspects except that the bend and shoulder displacement are to the outside of the arena rather than the inside. This movement really does help the cob learn to open his shoulders more in the movement as the

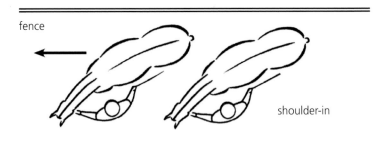

fence

shoulder-in

fence

counter shoulder-in

Shoulder-in and counter shoulder-in.

open side 'allows' more movement that way (whereas in true shoulder-in the shoulder has the wall there, which some say prevents this opening of the shoulder). In all key areas, the requirements are the same as for shoulder-in, except the positioning is reversed.

BENEFITS

In developing shoulder-in and counter shoulder-in in-hand, you are further developing the level of bend your cob is able to give you while maintaining balance off the shoulders. Of course the shoulder on the inside of the bend must not fall in but, at the same time, the shoulders should not be allowed to bulge out. This really does give you, as trainer, true control of your cob's shoulders while at the same time giving you the ability to engage and gymnasticize the inside (to the bend) hind leg. Working both the shoulder-in and the counter shoulder-in will assist with suppleness and bend as well as giving a softness in the bend that may not have been present previously. This softness into the bend and contact, if being assessed by a trained dressage judge, would give you higher marks in the 'submission' element at the bottom of your sheet.

As previously mentioned, the counter shoulder-in really teaches your cob to open his shoulders as he abducts his outside foreleg towards the middle of the arena. Collection is a direct result of practising and perfecting this exercise both in-hand and ridden.

PREREQUISITES

Shoulder-in and its partner the counter shoulder-in should only be started once your cob can perform the giravolta and a couple of steps out of the giravolta in leg-yield while maintaining the speed as set by you, staying soft in the contact and maintaining the established balance off the shoulders. If you can put together a short sequence of movements using the giravolta and leg-yield without any major losses of balance then you can be sure that your cob is ready to start the two exercises. With the giravolta and leg-yield established, the shoulder-in will be easily picked up by your cob; indeed the aids are more or less established.

SEQUENCE OF DEVELOPMENT

Developing Shoulder-In

To develop the shoulder-in, stand your cob at the track on the left rein with you standing in the default position (*see* Chapter 1) on his left-hand side. Establish inside flexion and softness to the contact and then ask your cob to step forward. Once your cob has stepped forward, place your right hand on his shoulder and ask for some balance of the inside shoulder. Again, once this is established, move your right hand just a little further back and pulse just behind the shoulder – or even slightly further back towards where the girth of a saddle would go. Pulse here, asking for a little more bend. As you are pulsing with your right hand, make sure there is still a feeling down the rein in that hand. The inside hand maintains inside flexion and softness, but not to the extent that you get too much neck bend. If you do get too much neck bend (which is more likely on his less stiff side), take a little more outside rein, which crosses his withers. The pulsing of the outside rein as it crosses his withers not only straightens the neck bend a little; it also pushes his shoulders in. Both actions are favourable in this situation. If he does not respond to your right hand's pulsing by offering a little more bend

Showing the use of the driving hand. I have already softened Ketchup at the base of her neck and at the shoulder. Now I am working behind the shoulder to develop greater bend.

and sideways stepping, make sure you do not push into your cob, as all he'll do is push back. Instead, sharpen up the pulses and make sure there is a clear release, which will stop him pushing back to you. If this does not work, use the whip with little taps to move his middle part out. As soon as you get the correct positioning and your cob offers one or two steps, stop and praise him.

When you can achieve two or three steps consistently while maintaining bend, flexion, softness and control over the speed, you can take the shoulder-in further along the track, at first for five or six steps, remembering to respond to each good attempt with praise, and to every increase in distance with more praise! Soon you will be able to maintain this for a full long side of a 40m arena.

As always, this work must be developed equally on both reins to develop a truly ambidextrous cob that can go equally on each rein.

Once developed equally on both reins, and the shoulder-in can be maintained for a full long side of a 40m arena (or the equivalent distance in a large arena), you can take your shoulder-in for a little jog. Once the movement is established, quicken your own pace while asking your cob to step up to a shortened trot. You may need to lose some angle in the transition to trot for the first couple of attempts, and only maintain it for three or four steps initially. Remember to praise your

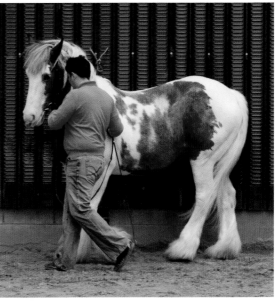

ABOVE LEFT Here I am asking Ketchup to give inside flexion. My driving hand is directly above her forearm at her shoulder. I am asking her to balance a little more off the shoulder for better shoulder-in balance and increased collection.

ABOVE RIGHT Improved balance is shown in her higher outline and engaged hind leg. I have started to move my hand back here to develop greater bend now that I have taken her balance off the shoulder.

LEFT The result. Lovely balance, bend and carriage.

cob for his efforts. If balance and softness are lost, stop and re-establish these qualities in walk before trying again. Allow the loss of bend and shoulder-in angle in the first few attempts and, so long as balance and the soft inside flexion are not lost, you can press for the shoulder-in angle a little more once the shortened trot is established.

Soon you will find that you can press your cob to maintain the angle and bend established in the walk shoulder-in into his shoulder-in in shortened trot. Once you are at this stage, on both reins, you

Another view of the shoulder-in in-hand.

ABOVE LEFT Coming through the corner onto the long side. I have started to bring Ketchup's shoulders off the track and have asked her to balance off her shoulders.

ABOVE RIGHT Further down the track in a fully established three-track shoulder-in.

can incorporate the shoulder-in into your transition sequences, which will further develop collection, lightness and strength in your cob's hindquarters.

Developing Counter Shoulder-In

To work on counter shoulder-in, the basic steps are identical to those explained above, except that you position your cob as though (for example) on the right rein, but with you positioned still on the left, now between the wall and your cob. In some ways the counter shoulder-in can be easier to establish because you can use the wall to stop your cob pushing too much forward and, by flexing him towards the wall, you will establish the angle much more easily as well as more quickly. So, positioned on the left-hand side of your cob, ask for left flexion with your left hand, press his shoulders out to the right slightly with your right hand in a pulsing action and then ask for him to walk on. Once in walk, move your right hand back and press for a little more angle and bend. You should find these quickly become established in counter shoulder-in. The progression of steps in the training sequence

LEFT In counter shoulder-in you can use the wall or fence to your advantage. If your cob is very strong in shoulder-in, then using the wall in counter shoulder-in will help to keep the balance without being dragged around like a rag doll.

CENTRE A little more bend and collection shown here.

RIGHT Nice use of Ketchup's off (right) hind leg.

is now identical to those described for shoulder-in. Start to develop longer and longer sequences of counter shoulder-in before trying it in a shortened trot.

You will need to continue practising both shoulder-in and counter shoulder-in as they will, in turn, be used to develop renvers and travers respectively in due course.

 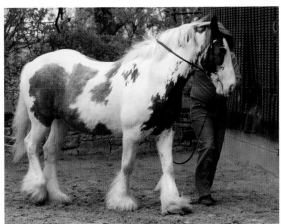

Another view of counter shoulder-in.

A further view, showing better bend and shoulder balance and, although Ketchup could be rounder still, her outline is better here than in the previous image.

CHAPTER EIGHT

In-Hand Travers, Renvers and Half-Pass

So you now have control over your cob's shoulders, you can engage his inside hind leg and move him sideways away from the direction of the bend. Now, for a truly supple, manoeuvrable cob, you'll need to control his quarters much more directly and engage his outside hind leg in a much more sophisticated way, as well as teaching him to travel sideways while maintaining a bend into the direction of travel. The combined effects are much more difficult for your cob because he needs to stretch so much more on his outside while, at the same time, stepping over towards his centre with the outside legs.

The travers, renvers and half-pass are identical movements in terms of biomechanics: the only major difference is the position in the school in which they are practised, and which line of movement is being followed.

What are Travers, Renvers and Half-Pass?

Travers

Travers is basically a quarters-in exercise. It is usually practised on the track with inside bend. The cob's forehand is kept on the track and the quarters are pushed in on an inner track, preferably so that your cob is on four tracks. Although in training three tracks is a good intermediate form, in reality the gymnastic effect is not complete until your cob can

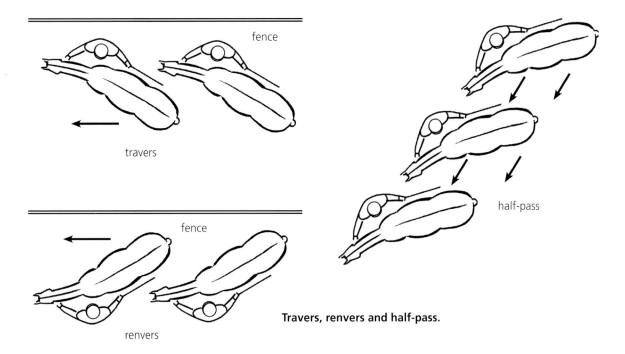

Travers, renvers and half-pass.

perfect the movement on four tracks. A clear requisite is the bend to the inside, which keeps the forehand looking straight forward down the track. The forehand itself should not be displaced to the inside. If it is, it is more of a leg-yield rather than a true travers.

Ketchup showing travers. Shoulders on the track, quarters pushed to the inside, with the bend in the direction of travel.

61

Renvers

The relationship of renvers to travers is the same as the relationship of shoulder-in to the counter shoulder-in. Basically, if you picture travers on the left rein, then move the fence from the outside of the cob to the inside, you have renvers on the right rein. So in renvers, your cob will be positioned with his shoulders to the inside but the bend will be to the outside.

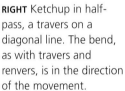

LEFT Ketchup in a clear renvers. Her quarters remain on the track. Her shoulders are brought in but her bend and flexion are to the outside so she is looking down the track rather than to the inside.

RIGHT Ketchup in half-pass, a travers on a diagonal line. The bend, as with travers and renvers, is in the direction of the movement.

Half-Pass

Half-pass is a specific type of travers, which is ridden across a diagonal line. Imagine a fence line positioned across the diagonal in the arena. Then imagine a travers ridden across this diagonal line. This is essentially what half-pass is. The cob is moving forward and sideways with the bend clearly into the direction of the movement, with the shoulders leading the movement but with the quarters clearly stepping into the movement as well.

BENEFITS

These movements engage the cob's outside hind leg. Because he is moving sideways into the direction of bend, the stretch on the outside of your cob's body creates tone and develops greater strength across the loins (especially on the outside), as well as the articulation of the outside foreleg and shoulder. This series of movements creates a more advanced form of collection and engagement.

PREREQUISITES

Successful schooling in both shoulder-in and counter shoulder-in are essential for the development of these movements, as travers is developed from the counter shoulder-in and renvers is developed from the shoulder-in. The half-pass is the culmination of both of these exercises.

SEQUENCE OF DEVELOPMENT

As the relationship between the travers and the counter shoulder-in is the same as the relationship between the shoulder-in and the renvers, the development is identical and must be perfected on both reins.

These exercises involve a switch of flexion and bend so, first of all, it would be wise to practise the change of flexion described in Chapter 2.

Developing Renvers

Let's start with a shoulder-in on the left rein. Keeping your cob in the shoulder-in position, halt him and, once in halt, change the flexion from the inside to the outside while maintaining the angle of his body. Make sure you keep his shoulders pushing in towards you by keeping your body back so as not to push his shoulders back to the track. Using the rein that is over your cob's neck (in this case the right rein), slip the rein back towards the withers, even behind the withers. This will allow a change of flexion much more easily and (especially if you can slip it back behind your cob's withers) it will help your cob use his whole forehand to change the bend and flexion. Once you have switched flexion, pick up walk again. When you can successfully switch his flexion in this way, he is performing renvers. One or two steps are enough before praising him, then you can build on this with more and more steps.

If your cob loses angle in the change of flexion it can help if you position yourself further back behind his shoulder while maintaining more demanding pulsations behind where the girth would go.

The exercise can then be built upon in two different ways. First, by increasing the number of steps asked for, and second, by asking for

ABOVE LEFT Here, from the shoulder-in, I am changing Ketchup's flexion so she looks into the movement down the track. Notice how I have taken my hand off the bit ring and how I am lengthening that rein.

ABOVE RIGHT Here we are in the middle of changing the flexion. Notice how Ketchup has tilted her head. This could be a sign of stiffness, or it could be a sign that I have been too slow at allowing that left rein to stretch. Also notice the increased angle from a three-track shoulder-in to a four-track renvers.

LEFT The tilt was only momentary. Here Ketchup is in a full renvers.

a change of bend and flexion while still walking. It can be difficult to synchronize the change of aids while in movement, but if you take your time the following tips should help. On the left rein, first slow the walk by slowing your steps and expecting your cob to accommodate your change of speed. Stop asking for the inside flexion with your left hand and increase the vibration down the right rein over your cob's withers. As you do this, step back a little behind your cob's shoulder as you move your right hand back a little while pulsing to maintain the angle and positioning. Of course, this needs to be developed on both reins.

Start of renvers, lacking displacement and bend.

Improving bend.

Full renvers.

Developing Travers

Once the shoulder-in can be turned into renvers, the counter shoulder-in can be turned into travers using exactly the same methods. On the right rein, with you standing on the outside of your cob, ask for counter shoulder-in. When you are ready you need to halt in exactly the same way as described above to switch flexion – this time from the outside to the inside. However, if your cob has understood the previous exercise you may find this step unnecessary, in which case a change of flexion while walking may be more appropriate. The change of aids is exactly as mentioned above.

RIGHT From the counter shoulder-in (as seen on page 59), the flexion is switched. Instead of looking out as in the counter shoulder-in, Ketchup is now looking down the track in the direction of movement.

FAR RIGHT After the change of flexion and bend, Ketchup continues in a nice travers down the track.

PHOTOS BELOW More views of travers.

Developing Half-Pass

Once you can turn shoulder-in into renvers, and counter shoulder-in into travers, you are ready to take these movements onto a diagonal line and school the half-pass. To school the half-pass you need to be on the outside of your cob. So, on the right rein with you on the outside (left-hand side of your cob), turn your cob down the centre line. Halt when you have turned so you can organize yourself. With your right hand, ask for right flexion and when ready walk on, maintaining the right flexion using the right rein, which is crossing over your cob's back just behind his withers. Your right hand, holding on to this rein, should drop back

 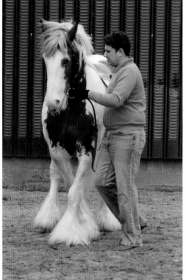 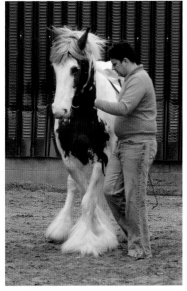

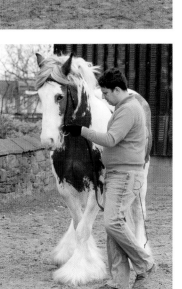

ABOVE LEFT From the turn across the school I am initiating the half-pass. Here Ketchup has pushed sideways with her quarters. I am now trying to catch up with her shoulders.

ABOVE CENTRE Now that the shoulders are in a better alignment, we can continue with the half-pass.

ABOVE RIGHT Now it is my body language that is taking Ketchup forward and sideways in the half-pass.

BOTTOM ROW Approaching the track.

slightly and be pulsing on your cob's side close to where a rider's leg would be. It pulses when the hind leg on that side is raised, as this is when your aid can affect its trajectory. These two aids combined will keep your cob in the correct flexion, while maintaining the necessary displacement of the quarters. It is a function of your body language and positioning to move your cob diagonally across into a half-pass, so use your stepping direction to move across the front of your cob into the direction you want to travel. By walking across your cob's shoulder, you are in effect blocking forward motion and redirecting your cob sideways and into a half-pass, thereby moving your cob on a diagonal line heading back to the track. One or two steps will be enough before praising. Build up the steps until your cob can half-pass from the centre line back to the track, maintaining balance and form on both reins.

Think about keeping your cob's shoulders leading across this movement so that, when viewed from the front, your cob's quarters never lead the movement. To help with this, think first of all about taking his shoulders over into the half-pass; they are the priority. If you just concentrate on taking the quarters sideways you will inevitably push the quarters too far sideways and make them lead the movement. Once you have the shoulders moving, you can then take your pulsing hand a little further back to take his whole body 'with them'.

As with all other movements mentioned so far, this series can and should also be developed in the shortened trot, using the same methods described earlier.

....

CHAPTER NINE

In-Hand Piaffe

Many of the exercises so far have dealt with lateral suppleness along with longitudinal suppleness and softness. Up until now we have thought about developing this suppleness alongside gentle collection exercises such as the various lateral movements, but now our focus is changing. We are now starting to think about developing real strength in the hindquarters. Not just in the hind leg but also up into the hip and around your cob's pelvis and sacroiliac region.

What is Piaffe?

Piaffe is the most collected form of trot. It is a form of trot that takes on a distinctive posture with a tilted pelvis, extra flexion in all the hind leg joints, a rounded back and the cob being 'on the bit' with his poll high, nose just in front of the vertical. The cob should maintain the diagonal stepping that is so distinctive of the trot, while shortening the steps until the piaffe is almost completely on the spot. I always think of it as a lively bubbly movement akin to the gentle fizz of a sparkling drink. It is the movement that really illustrates the cob's 'uphill' quality, as not only do the hindquarters sit but, as a consequence, the forefeet get lighter and the image is that they 'levitate' somewhat and only just touch down.

Ketchup in piaffe: a highly collected trot on the spot. You can see that her diagonal pair (left foreleg, right hind leg) are lifted together.

BENEFITS

This movement engages the cob's hind legs to the ultimate level without then practising airs above the ground. Indeed, in the classical schools, the piaffe was used as a preparation for the airs above the ground, the strengthening it develops in the hindquarters enabling the horse to perform exercises such as the levade, and the various jumps. As well as developing strength in the hindquarters, the piaffe enhances and develops many of the conditioning exercises practised so far. As he works towards the piaffe, your cob will tuck his pelvis under much more, dropping his tail lower by working, contracting and toning his deep abdominal core muscles, rather like a tummy crunch in humans. In tilting his pelvis, he will also round and stretch his back and, while his hind legs step under his body mass, he will lighten his forehand. This rounded back will arch from his tilted pelvis to his shoulders, then to his poll. The 'uphill' attitude of the piaffe is achieved by some isometric action of the long topline muscles, which pull the weight of the forehand back over the hindquarters. This strengthening of the hindquarters, along with redistribution of weight and balance, will enable him to carry his weight with his hind legs rather than just pushing forward with them.

PREREQUISITES

The development of the piaffe should be started and practised along-side the development of the higher-level lateral movements such as half-pass. Your cob must be able to maintain balance in-hand, with slight inside flexion in walk, shortened trot and rein-back. He should also be able to show giravolta, engaging lateral steps and some passable shoulder-in steps in walk and shortened trot.

SEQUENCE OF DEVELOPMENT

Piaffe is developed out of the repeated rein-back to trot transitions. With this in mind, it is time to start repeated rein-back, trot, rein-back exercises around the school. At first you'll need to have quite a few trot strides to establish balance and harmony – maybe fifteen or even twenty (and, if necessary, more). Then halt, rein-back about four or five steps, then go forward to trot. To begin with, all these transitions should be progressive. Your cob must maintain softness throughout, so if it is lost stop, re-establish his soft contact and start again with a little more focus on the balance and softness. If he manages these transitions while maintaining the softness and harmony, stop and praise him.

First moment of the rein-back that precedes the trot transition. You can already see how the rein-back positively affects the cob's posture.

Soon, the trot strides can be limited to ten or twelve, moving directly into increasingly responsive halt transitions (which, while 'prompt', should still maintain harmony and should not be abrupt). Following the halt, rein-back six steps and then move straight forward into trot. When you repeat these exercises, the trot steps should naturally shorten and heighten. So allow this to happen, accommodating the shortened strides by slowing down yourself. When you notice this shortening, reward your cob for his good efforts.

The visibly shortened trot out of the rein-back is the foundation upon which we will build the piaffe.

Begin to shorten the trot even more, especially for the first three or four steps directly out of the rein-back. Now might be the time to develop a piaffe aid with your whip: I always use this in the rhythm I am looking for in the piaffe. Slight taps of the whip over the cob's hips, just behind the stifle, or on the upper thigh should help. Try each of these and find out which your cob responds to best.

Soon you should be able to ask for a 'forward' step out of the rein-back while maintaining a position a little more on the spot. As soon as your cob gives a diagonal step on the spot, stop and reward him. This is the key to getting him to understand. These steps should be slightly forward (up to about 22cm apart) and are called the half-steps. Do not think about keeping these piaffe half-steps on the spot – that is for a year or two down the line. For now, think of building the piaffe half-steps step by step. First ask for one step, then two, and build from there.

While maintaining the diagonalized stepping, the piaffe is developed. Here we see the half-steps developing, where the cob is allowed to step forward a little at each step.

The piaffe more or less on the spot, with a more 'uphill' frame and engaged hind legs.

The key now is time. By this I mean not days, not even weeks; we are thinking long-term – more like months and even years. So do not be in a rush to build these steps. I cannot stress this enough: *do not* ask for too much too soon.

When two or three steps can be offered successfully, try this sequence again but in a shoulder-in position, as this further strengthens each hind leg in turn. As a direct consequence of this positioning, you should also notice that your cob's shoulders lighten further.

Other variations would be to ask your cob to perform a giravolta, or a lateral engaging step back to the track, and then ask for a diagonalized half-step or two of piaffe, or to arrive back at the track after a half-pass in walk and then press for a diagonalized step when reaching the track.

Once you have practised piaffe half-steps for a long period and can ask for about six or seven steps, you can then shorten the steps further and ask your cob to be even more on the spot for one or two steps, then back out into the half steps. This foundation can then be built on to develop up to four steps a little more on the spot, with about a hoof width between each step.

....

CHAPTER TEN

In-Hand Passage and Spanish Walk

Passage is one of the hallmarks of advanced dressage and high school equitation. For many it is one of those movements that they feel to be beyond their capabilities, or beyond the talents of their cob. It is through the Spanish walk and its ability to loosen the shoulders and create a stylized step that passage becomes possible.

What is the Spanish Walk?

Because the Spanish walk is used here to develop the passage, we shall work through the Spanish walk first. Spanish walk is a clear four-beat walk where the actions of the forelegs become so stylized that the leg is brought out, lifted well beyond its normal height and the knee

PHOTOS BELOW Ketchup showing a Spanish walk step. Her foreleg is outstretched while her hind leg is lifted and about to step under.

straightened with each step. It is rather like a goose-step without the walk rhythm getting too quick.

BENEFITS

This exercise mainly works the cob's shoulders but, from the handler's point of view, it also gives control over the rhythm and articulation of the forelegs' joints and in the long run it will give the handler control of cadence, especially when this exercise is transferred to ridden work.

PREREQUISITES

To develop the Spanish walk the basics of halt and walk on should be well established. I find it useful to have the giravolta established as well, and your cob should be able to give a step or two of leg-yielding with good engagement. Therefore work towards Spanish walk can parallel the work done in establishing the lateral movements. Spanish walk takes time to establish and it may be months before a polished sequence of Spanish walk steps will be produced.

SEQUENCE OF DEVELOPMENT

The first step in working towards the Spanish walk is getting your cob to react to the instructions of the whip by lifting his foreleg to a little tickle of the whip. This phase needs to be very experimental from the trainer's point of view. You may need to experiment with where on the cob's foreleg you ask for him to lift, but you may also need to experiment with what kind of pressure you put on. Some cobs respond well to a 'tickle', with the schooling whip lightly brushing around the leg; others respond better to a tap, or even a poke. Make sure you stand to the side of your cob; never stand in front of him otherwise he could accidently bash into you! At this stage work the foreleg closest to you, and make sure you switch sides to work his other foreleg. As soon as your cob moves the leg in response to the stimulus from the whip, reward him. Once he makes the link between the stimulus and his action you'll be halfway there, and the only way to do that is to reward him for any positive reactions. This must be done with both legs. Voice commands such as saying 'lift' or 'leg' also help at this stage.

At first, the raising of the foreleg will be low and not that expressive. As long as there is a reaction, be happy with your cob's effort.

Once your cob responds every time you ask him to lift his leg (and this only needs to be a bend at the knee and then placing the leg back down) you can begin to take the step 'for a walk'. To do this, ask for a leg lift, and then ask your cob to walk a step, then ask for a leg lift again, keeping the leg lifts to one particular leg at any one time. Initially you need to do one step at a time, then halt, then ask for a leg lift and then repeat. Of course this should be done with both legs, but working only a single leg at any one time.

Here you can see me raising my hand to aid down the rein at the same time as aiding with the whip on Ketchup's forearm.

At this point you could also develop another aid to lifting the leg. To make it easy to transfer over to ridden work, I teach my cobs to lift a leg to pressure down the rein on the same side as the leg I want my cob to lift. To do this, make an upward check on the rein as you ask for the leg to be lifted. As long as you always use the same upward check on the rein as you ask for the leg to be lifted, your cob will soon make the connection and respond to the rein alone. Now you can start to work not only the leg closest to you, but also the leg on the other side as well. Having the ability to work the leg on the far side will be necessary shortly when you want consecutive Spanish walk steps.

Soon you will probably find that your cob will start to lift the leg higher and keep it in the air for longer. This is to be encouraged. If he does not do this, you can start to ask for him to pick up his leg higher and for longer by aiding for a longer time or correcting him if he puts his leg down too soon. Hold off rewarding him until he has kept his leg in the air for longer, or brings his leg up higher.

Once these increasingly stylized steps are occurring consistently you can begin to ask for both legs to work consecutively. This requires quick action on your part and is often easier if you work the leg furthest away from you and then switch to the leg nearest to you. To do this you need to switch the instructions quite quickly from the outside

Here I am asking for a little extra expression. As shown on the front cover, Ketchup is more than able to have a fully horizontal foreleg in her Spanish Walk (indeed, her foreleg is sometimes raised above horizontal).

rein and using the whip on the outside leg to raising the inside hand and using the whip on the inside leg. First, try one left-right Spanish walk step.

From here on, Spanish walk is easy to build up. You simply have to add more and loftier steps in a sequence, but you should not do too many as they are taxing for the cob. I tend to do no more than six or seven at any one time. Once you are at this stage, you can now concentrate on maintaining rhythm so that your cob does not 'steam on' ahead.

Consecutive steps of Spanish walk.

Better Spanish walk steps here; Ketchup is showing a much more 'uphill frame' and in each photo here the hind legs are looking more active than in the photos above.

What is Passage?

Passage is a highly stylized, cadenced trot with a distinctive rhythm, flexion of the joints and suspension of the limbs. In nature it is produced in excitement but in terms of training, we want to produce it in a calm and gentle environment. If, when I am describing passage, people look at me with a blank face, I always describe it as a trot with a gazelle-like prance. This often clarifies what we are after.

BENEFITS

Passage combines the strength requirements of the piaffe with the power recoil of extended trot and shoulder mobility of the Spanish walk. In many ways it is the culmination of all this work: collection as well as extension, cadence and rhythm.

PREREQUISITES

Piaffe must be started before passage is taught. If passage is taught first, your cob may use this stylized trot as an escape from the ultimate collection in piaffe. The rudimentary stages of Spanish walk – raising a leg on command – must be established, though the full Spanish walk is not necessary in order to begin passage.

SEQUENCE OF DEVELOPMENT

Once your cob is able to raise a leg on command, you can begin to ask for a shortened trot after your cob has given you a raised leg. Making sure you are positioned to the side in your in-hand default position, take your time through the transitions and asking for the elevated step. Initially return to halt before asking for the elevated step.

Once your cob is happy with this exercise, you can begin to ask for the elevated step during the shortened trot. In this situation, staying to the side of your cob, ask him for an elevated trot step when the foreleg closest to you is grounded. This gives him time to think about how to organize his legs. You may need to ask a few times before he gives an elevated step. Keep looking out for it and, as soon as he gives you a slightly more elevated step, stop and praise him. Keep asking for single

CLOCKWISE FROM ABOVE
How we prepare for the passage in-hand.

elevated steps on both reins until he is giving them to you more con-sistently and within a step or two of asking.

Once he is more consistent in giving these single elevated steps on each rein, it is time to ask for repeated elevated steps (on single legs). At this stage, if your cob is working through Spanish walk, he may even offer consecutive steps with both legs. If he does, stop and praise him. That is a big success. Because of the speed of the movements in trot, it is often difficult to get more than a step or two, so once you are able to get a couple of elevated steps, passage work can commence ridden.

Although ridden passage training can now be started, there are still a few exercises that can help the passage. Because piaffe will be achievable if you are schooling your cob at this level, you can begin to work through piaffe to passage transitions. Establish piaffe as you would normally on whichever rein is easier for you. Ask for a few steps of piaffe, with your body positioned in your usual place for piaffe, with the whip towards the quarters; then, when you are ready, reposition the whip to ask for lofty steps out of piaffe. Take your time over the repositioning of the whip so you do not worry your cob. At the moment of the switch, remember to move forward with your cob once he steps out into the loftier steps. And again, remember to praise him when he gives you what you want. This helps to achieve a passage that is well engaged behind, and begins to teach those all-important piaffe-passage-piaffe transitions.

INTRODUCTION
TO RIDDEN WORK

Your in-hand work is the foundation of your cob's schooling and education. It is your riding position and the way you interact with your cob that become your stable base from which your ridden schooling will develop. A shaky position, poor interaction and faulty absorption of your cob's movement will detract from the stable base and become a hindrance to your progress as a rider, as well as your cob's progress in his schooling. This section starts with you, your position and your interaction with your cob's movement. Once these qualities are honed to a fine standard, you can then build on the foundation stones already laid by the groundwork to school your cob to higher levels. The truth of this will be emphasized at the start of the following chapters, where the rider's prerequisite qualities are summarized, along with those of the cob. You will see that, although there are some qualities that are especially pertinent to the exercises under discussion, those of correct position, appropriate contact and good rapport are highlighted time and again, as reminders of how important they are to all work.

All the movements necessary for suppling, collection and building strength are outlined in the following chapters.

CHAPTER ELEVEN

The Rider's Position

So far we have dealt with training your cob in-hand. Now it is time to translate what you and your cob have learned to ridden work and, of course, this has to start with your position and your ridden interaction with your cob. Your position is your default but, as you will soon realize, this is not a static posture, but a dynamic position that allows you to interact safely with your cob's movement and to move with him in a manner that can influence his way of going as positively as possible.

What is the Correct Rider's Position?

It is widely documented what a rider's correct position should be. The correct classical position is a vertical one in which an imaginary line, perpendicular to the ground, dissects the rider's body through the crown, ears, shoulders, hips and heels. This is the ideal, but it is elusive – our task is to come as close to this as possible. (Many instructors teach position only: this is short-sighted because it oversimplifies riding to a static ideal, whereas riding takes place in motion.) From this classical position you are ideally placed to absorb your cob's movements as closely and as easily as possible. Within this position the most important part is the orientation of the pelvis. An upright pelvis with the two seat bones pointing directly down is essential for the ridden work and will be the first exercise we address.

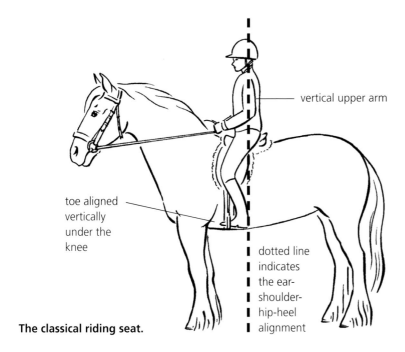

vertical upper arm

toe aligned
vertically
under the
knee

dotted line
indicates
the ear-
shoulder-
hip-heel
alignment

The classical riding seat.

BENEFITS

We have already touched on the interaction benefits of the correct
classical position. Other benefits include a stable base that enhances
security and balance and facilitates the application of understandable
aids to your cob. And let's not forget that elegance – one of the hallmarks of classical riding – will be another of the benefits.

SEQUENCE OF DEVELOPMENT THROUGH EXERCISE

Some of the following exercises can be practised on a wooden saddle
horse, a peanut gym/physio ball, or a hard stool or equivalent. Some
can be done quickly while mounted on your cob as mini checkpoints.
The exercises outlined are those I consider most helpful in achieving
an effective position. More detailed descriptions of the rider's position
can be found in my earlier book, *Cobs Can!*

The Upright Pelvis

As described earlier, the upright pelvis is the most essential aspect of a
successful riding position. To achieve this you need to become aware of
the shape of the rocker-like ischia or seat bones. To do this it is helpful

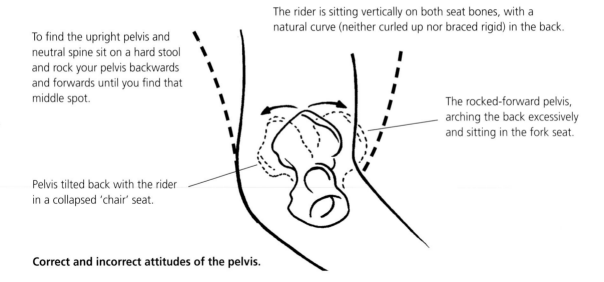

To find the upright pelvis and neutral spine sit on a hard stool and rock your pelvis backwards and forwards until you find that middle spot.

The rider is sitting vertically on both seat bones, with a natural curve (neither curled up nor braced rigid) in the back.

The rocked-forward pelvis, arching the back excessively and sitting in the fork seat.

Pelvis tilted back with the rider in a collapsed 'chair' seat.

Correct and incorrect attitudes of the pelvis.

to sit on a level stool, or on the edge of a hard chair, with your knees bent and your feet resting lightly on the floor.

Become aware of what you are sitting on. The movement you will make is a rocking action of your pelvis forward and back. To do this you will need to go from arching your back, through the full range of movement to rounding your back. As you rock from position to position be aware of how this feels in and around your seat bones.

The ideal position is exactly between the two extremes. Gradually centralize the rocking action, making sure not to go so far each way until you reach your central point. You should feel as though your seat bones are resting in a central level point. If you have a mirror handy, or a friend with a camera, check in the mirror or image that your pelvis looks upright and that your back shows its natural curve, with your shoulders directly above your hips.

Remember this position, taking a mental snapshot of how it feels, and then try to replicate it with the help of the same exercises while in the saddle.

Absorbing the Movement in Walk and Trot

The following exercises will really help your mobility and control in absorbing the movements in the gaits.

The 'Walk and Sitting Trot' Exercise This involves resting your whole body against a wall. Make sure your back, bottom and heels are against the wall. Bend your knees at the angle you would for riding, making sure your knee is no further forward than the front of your toes.

Flex your back forward so that the small of your back leaves the wall. Then straighten your back again and bring your pelvis back to upright. Do this a couple of times to limber up your lower back. Then try arching your back slightly, but this time taking one of your hips further forward than the other by arching one side of your back a little more than the other.

ABOVE LEFT Here the upright pelvis allows the correct position of back and legs. It is the neutral base from which you flex your back forward, never backwards, and allow your seat bones to advance unilaterally as the cob pushes up and forward with his back.

ABOVE RIGHT In sitting trot, my upper body is still inclined forward, far from ideal. Being pitched forward limits the use of your lower back when absorbing the movement with your seat. It will inevitably make you bounce.

RIGHT A better alignment, though still a couple of degrees forward of the ideal. It is not so forward that it is inhibiting the use of my back to absorb the bounce. In this photo my left seat bone is being pushed more up and forward by Ketchup's left hip – note that her right hip is low.

Now alternate your hips each time you flex your spine forward. It may be helpful to think of your hips as 'walking'. Once you are comfortable doing this, alter the speed by imagining walk speeds and trot speeds. Trot is often double the speed and with a little more back flexion too.

This exercise can also be done lying on the floor with your knees up, seated on a stool or even on the peanut physio ball. When practising the trot on the physio ball add a bit of bounce to make it more realistic.

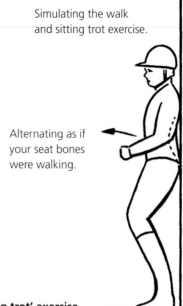

Simulating the walk and sitting trot exercise.

Alternating as if your seat bones were walking.

The 'walk and sitting trot' exercise.

The Correct Rising Trot Most riders ride at trot with their shoulders far too upright, vertically aligned above the hips. The problem with this comes with the inevitable forward momentum of the trot combined with most riders' lack of strength in their core. A totally upright, vertical position in the rising trot will inevitably result in the rider becoming left behind the movement. So the first thing I ask riders to do is to fold the upper body forward from the hips. Be sure that, when you do this, you do not hollow your back. As long as the angle of your thigh is such that your knee is pretty much vertically above the front of your toe, as in the correct classical position, the rise should not be too much of a problem, as the movement of your cob will lift your pelvis and rock it forward towards the pommel of the saddle. Think of the movement as rocking forward rather than lifting up. If your cob has a lot of natural impulsion, he may rock your pelvis forward to the point where your body now looks upright. If your cob does not push your pelvis this far, do not force it: only go as far as your cob pushes you. As he builds his impulsion your cob will rock your pelvis further forward. The key is only to go as far as his movement rocks you. As you return to the seated position, fold again from the hips and bring your seat bones back into the saddle. Make sure they do come back to the saddle fully; hovering/light seat in rising trot is rarely useful.

ABOVE LEFT The correct alignment for the sitting phase of the rising trot. Note that the upper body is inclined forward of the vertical and so, too, are the seat bones, which are ready to receive the power of the cob's back propelling them up and forward.

ABOVE RIGHT Rising off the cob's back. Note it is not an excessive rise. Rather, it is more appropriate to think of going to where your cob pushes you. Ideally, my foot should have remained more parallel to the ground.

RIGHT In this rise, owing to increased impulsion from Ketchup, I have risen rather higher than earlier, not because I have tried hard but more because she has pushed me there. My lower leg is much better here.

Absorbing the Movement in Canter

It is usually far easier to develop the seat in canter than in sitting trot. The first thing to understand is that, in the absorption of the canter, there is no backward movement of the shoulders. Think more of your shoulders going up and down. So first revisit the 'walk and sitting trot'

ABOVE LEFT The ideal position in the canter. If you can maintain a supple lower back and supple following hips in canter, you appear to remain still.

ABOVE RIGHT Even at the lowest part of the canter stride you need to appear vertical. By allowing your back to flex forward you can achieve this. It is at this point that most riders rock to well behind the vertical. If you do rock behind the vertical you will inevitably push your cob more onto the forehand at this vulnerable time.

RIGHT Ideally you would still want to be upright here. However, as you can see, I have rocked forward with my shoulders. Not at all ideal, but tipping forward is my major fault in my riding. Instead of using my deep core muscles to straighten my back and bring my pelvis back up to upright, I have rocked forward. Work in progress!

exercise described above, resting your upper body and heels against the wall and, with bent knees, practise for a while allowing your upper body to stretch upwards, slowly at first and then later in a rhythm similar to your cob's canter. Think 'stretch, stretch, stretch.'

When you are comfortable with this, at the same time as you think 'stretch', allow the top of your pelvis to tip forward slightly. Remember to come back to the neutral position in between the stretches. Initially, take your time, making the movements slower than you would for a true canter on your cob, and only come up to full speed when you are comfortable with all the movements involved.

Once you are at the stage of working these movements within an imagined canter rhythm, draw your attention to the top of your hips, continuing with the movements described. As canter has a distinct direction, your inside hip will advance and articulate the circle a little more than the other. Try to modify the movement so that your hip describes a backward circle. Usually it is the moment when you come back to neutral that needs attention, as the stretch of the upper body and the slight tip of the pelvis easily describe the front of the circle. So when coming back to neutral, feel as though you lift your hips up and back to the wall for that upright position so you really do get the full circle.

....

CHAPTER TWELVE

The Basic Exercises
of Ridden Work

The exercises that follow are a distillation of some of those detailed in my previous book, *Cobs Can!* These basic exercises not only build on the work you have achieved so far in-hand, but also provide the foundation stones for all later ridden work. They are essential to any progression and their basic forms relate to the 'go' aids, the 'stop' aids, the 'turn' aids and the flexion for softness down the rein.

The exercises build on all of these aspects and should be perfected through transitions between the gaits, and circles and turns in both directions before moving on to the more difficult work.

Responsiveness to the Aids

At this stage we are teaching our cob to be responsive to our basic aids for softening the jaw, for upward and downward transitions and for turning. This should not be hard work for cob or rider, though I know many instructors bamboozle people, making them think otherwise. At this stage we are beginning to unlock any evasions or blockages that inhibit the ridden work. These locks are usually misunderstandings between cob and rider and many of the 'solutions' involve the rider 'shouting louder', in much the same way that tourists shout louder in a language that the indigenous population does not understand at any volume! The correct solution is to explain as best you can, with clear, identifiable aids, and reward your cob when he responds correctly so he can make a link between the aid given and his response.

Forwardness

Logically, I believe that developing responsiveness starts with the forward aid. Without forwardness you have nothing – you need to develop a forward response to your leg aids. When I say 'forward', I do not mean running away from the leg; I mean moving comfortably and immediately away from the leg without rushing or tension. Once this is established the other basic exercises can be worked upon – the softness of the jaw, the downward aids and turning.

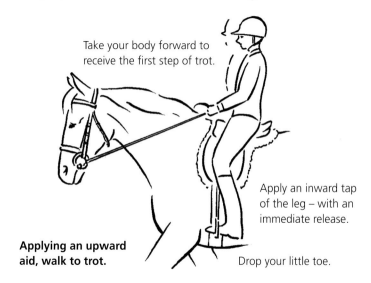

Take your body forward to receive the first step of trot.

Apply an inward tap of the leg – with an immediate release.

Applying an upward aid, walk to trot.

Drop your little toe.

The first thing to work on is applying the leg aids correctly. Too many people apply stronger and stronger leg aids with a kicking back heel. This only stiffens your cob's rib area and stops him being able to move forward correctly. Another aid commonly used is the aid that hugs, squeezes and is applied over a long time. This also stops your cob moving correctly because the 'release' that allows and rewards the forward movement just does not happen and therefore inhibits motion.

The correct leg aid should be considered a gentle (but can be stronger) touch, glance or tap with the inner calf. The heel has nothing to do with it. So, when seated in the saddle, check the alignment of your pelvis and check that your muscles are not tight or gripping, as this will inhibit any movement your cob will want to produce. The action is from

RIGHT The moment of the transition to trot. Note that my lower leg is still level; there is no kick back, the action involves lowering the little toe slightly with an inward nudge of the inner ankle. The heel has nothing to do with it. As Ketchup is moving forward I have eased my shoulders forward to receive the first step of trot and continue in rising trot. If your cob is 'forward' off the leg, moving directly into rising trot will cause no issue. Ensuring that your cob has a' forward' attitude by using the exercises described means you will just need to receive the forward trot step with your seat in the rising trot without needing to remain sitting and 'drive' more forwards.

a dropped leg, allowing gravity to pull the leg down to the ground. The lower leg wraps around the curve of your cob's barrel, and then, with a quick touch, you close your lower leg in a nutcracker action, at the same time rolling your calf forward, releasing your toe and knee as you do so. The movement is quick, gentle, but assertive. The release must be quick as it is this that allows and rewards the forward movement.

Here you can see the heel is directly below the hip, and the toe is directly below the knee. The toe is pointing forward and this stops the fleshy part of the calf being used in the leg aid, and prevents the leg twisting.

From a slightly different view, here we can see that the whole leg is draped gently around the cob. Lowering the little toe can help you to achieve this; it helps the lower leg stay quietly in place and stops the all-too-common 'kick back' when using your legs. Once in this position, all that is needed is an inward nudge, which releases immediately.

Make a few attempts at this, just asking your cob to move forward from halt. Keep your aiding light (remember light aids make a light cob; heavy aids make a heavy cob!) and if he responds by moving forward, reward him with a good pat. If he does not, be quick to back up your request with a tap of the schooling whip behind your leg – or even whack your boot a few times with the whip to bring his attention to your legs. You would be surprised how many horses I see (all types, not just cobs) that have become 'turned off' to the legs but respond happily once their attention has been brought to their rider's leg aids.

Repeated transitions of this basic type help create a 'forward' cob. One thing to watch, however, is to not overuse the legs. If you feel that you are pushing for every step, stop! If you feel this, the following exercise will help. From halt, apply the aid as above and ask your cob to walk on. Make sure you keep your leg released and do not apply your leg again while your cob walks on. Make sure your body 'goes forward' with your cob: allow your hips to swing with the undulations of his back and make sure to avoid inhibiting movement by tensing your thighs or fixing your body. If he slows or stops, use your leg again in a slightly sharper way, backing it up immediately with the schooling whip either behind the leg or on your boot and relax immediately. Repeat this each time he slows and soon he'll stay forward from light aids. By following these steps consistently you'll keep your cob forward-thinking and make him easier to ride without feeling as though you are pushing for every step.

From here, transitions to trot can be made in exactly the same way. Once in an energetic walk, apply the aid and be ready to receive the forward movement by taking your shoulders forward and receiving the first bounce of the trot. Again, make sure that your aid is not dull or hugging in its attitude. Allow your legs to drape round your cob's ribs before giving the tap with your calves. The sequence is therefore the same; if he responds, reward him. If he does not, back up your next leg aids with the whip, either behind the girth or on your boot.

As with the walk, do not apply the leg at every step – with a lethargic cob, that will result in him being pushed along by his rider. Instead, allow your legs to drape and allow your body to really move with him in the rising trot. If he slows, apply the leg aid in exactly the same way as described above, backing up the aid with the whip if required. We

Another moment of the walk to trot transition. Note that I am positioned to move up and forward with Ketchup's back.

are really looking for your cob to move freely forward at this stage. To achieve this, you need to be very clear to your cob what is acceptable and what is not and to be very consistent in achieving this.

Downward Aids

Once you have started to work on the exercises for moving your cob forward from the lighter leg aids, you'll soon realize that, to keep practising, you will need to make just as many downward transitions. These downward transitions are easy by comparison. All downward transitions are done in the same way. First, your core muscles must engage as though a small child were about to poke you in the stomach. Then you need to engage your inner thigh and buttock muscles as though hugging your cob's back. Hopefully, you can now see why the sustained hugging/squeezing leg aid does not produce upward transitions!

The strength with which you apply your aids varies from cob to cob. Also, some cobs listen to the upper thigh more, while others listen to the buttocks more. To find out which works best, you really need to experiment with your cob. The downward aid comes from the seat, not the hands, although they do play a part. The hands maintain a connection down the reins to the cob's mouth. Thinking of 'holding your cob's hand' in terms of maintaining a feel on his mouth prevents him from evading your seat aids by helping to contain his movement.

So, once you have found out how much thigh/buttock aiding your cob needs, and how much contact he needs down the reins to support the seat aids, you can make many upward and downward transitions to really get to him listen to you and to 'key in' to every signal you send.

The downward aids from rising trot to walk are just the same, except that the aiding should be applied at the moment of sitting and this, coupled with a slowing of the rising trot, brings quick results that are like magic to every rider who has not experienced them!

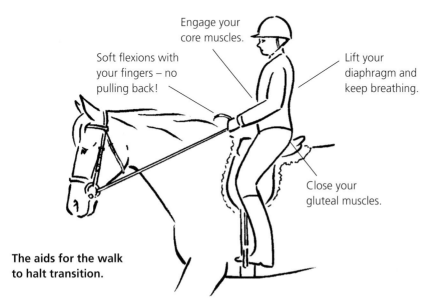

Soft flexions with your fingers – no pulling back!

Engage your core muscles.

Lift your diaphragm and keep breathing.

Close your gluteal muscles.

The aids for the walk to halt transition.

BELOW LEFT The moment I start using my seat to bring the trot down to the walk. Note the seat – in this case the use of the rising trot – is more dominant than the hands.

BELOW RIGHT The moment the walk happens: note that I am now sitting in a fully upright seat.

97

Flexion and Softness of the Jaw

Now that you can make upward and downward transitions in the walk and the trot from light aids, it is time to start riding these movements with a flexion in your cob's jaw and lightness down the reins. This is where our ridden work marries with our in-hand work. If your cob will lighten his mouth and release his jaw to small flexions in-hand, it will be so much easier when ridden.

Here Ketchup is 'against the hand'. So, with the little flexions from the fingers, I am asking her to soften her jaw and give a little more poll flexion.

The end result. Ketchup is softer to the contact, a little rounder and, though you cannot see it too well at this angle, she is giving very slight inside flexion.

From halt, shorten your reins to the point where you can easily feel your cob's mouth. Short reins allow you to release tension easily by slightly opening your fingers, but are easily used in a vibrating way by pulsing and tickling down the rein by closing your fingers. So, to ask your cob to soften his jaw, maintain the soft pressure down the rein and begin to vibrate it, initially to the inside of the bend that you are wanting to produce. Two or three gentle vibrations down one rein should be followed by the same on the other rein. Alternating like this, encourage your cob to unlock his jaw and release tension to produce a characteristic lightness in the reins.

After a couple of attempts to soften his jaw, release rein pressure by softening and releasing the rein by opening the fingers for a second. Then repeat, asking for the softness in the jaw. The release shows your cob that, once softness is achieved, you will be light to him; it is also used as a reward for the correct reaction to the flexions on the rein. As soon as he softens down the rein, release the pressure and reward your cob. At this stage he does not need to be 'round' and go 'on the bit' but he needs to be soft to your rein aids and this is where it starts.

Once your cob responds by softening his jaw, you can ask him to give flexion to the side, in this case to the inside. To do this, still at halt, once your cob is soft in his mouth, lift your inside hand slightly while increasing the tickles down the rein on that side. He'll turn his head to that side, showing you his eye and nostril. Again, reward him when he understands and responds correctly.

Now is the delicate time where you need to combine these flexions with the changes of balance in the transitions exercises we have already started. The key is to break it down easily for your cob so that the required response is easily achieved. First, start from halt with your cob flexed to the inside. Ask him to walk on and expect him to keep flexion to the inside and softness down the rein. If he does not, halt and try again, this time keeping a tickle down each rein consecutively during the transition. Repeat until he gives you a transition to walk while maintaining softness and inside flexion. Reward him when he achieves this.

Maintaining softness and inside flexion in the walk is achieved in exactly the same way as in the halt and should be easily maintained if you have worked through the halt to walk transition correctly.

Once softness and flexion can be maintained from halt to walk, and through the walk, transitions to trot should be attempted in exactly the same way. Keep the conversation going down both reins through the transition to the trot, and you should find the balance in trot will be much improved.

Never should the tension in the reins increase; never should there be backward pulling hands. The rider who achieves the best results has hands that are quick to release and let the cob out slightly. Throughout all of this, the rein aids have not changed – little tickles, vibrations or flexions down each rein independently. As soon as the cob responds, the rein becomes still and releases slightly. This is how you work towards true lightness and a cob that works in self-carriage.

ABOVE LEFT Here in the trot the cob is poking his nose and could have a little more inside flexion.

ABOVE RIGHT Here we have the same cob at a later date having learned these flexion exercises. They really polish the cob's way of going, giving him balance, poise and a more sophisticated way of moving.

School Movements and Transitions

Now you have all the skills in place to develop many of the preliminary school movements, the gymnastic effects of which will bring about greater roundness, balance off the shoulder, control, bend and rhythm. The easier exercises of circles build up to loops with their changes of bend and flexion. Walking the movements allows you time to understand the changes necessary, but it is in trot that your cob will achieve their athletic benefits. Once working in trot, do not go for too long before refreshing your cob's movement by making a transition down to walk for a few strides.

Inside Bend

To ride all of these movements you will need to ride with inside bend. Riding with flexion on the inside rein is the start, but is not quite enough. To achieve this you need to advance your inside hip, dropping your inside leg as a result and applying your inside leg forward at the girth with the swing of your cob's belly. This unilateral use of the leg, coupled with the advanced inside hip, helps your cob bend into

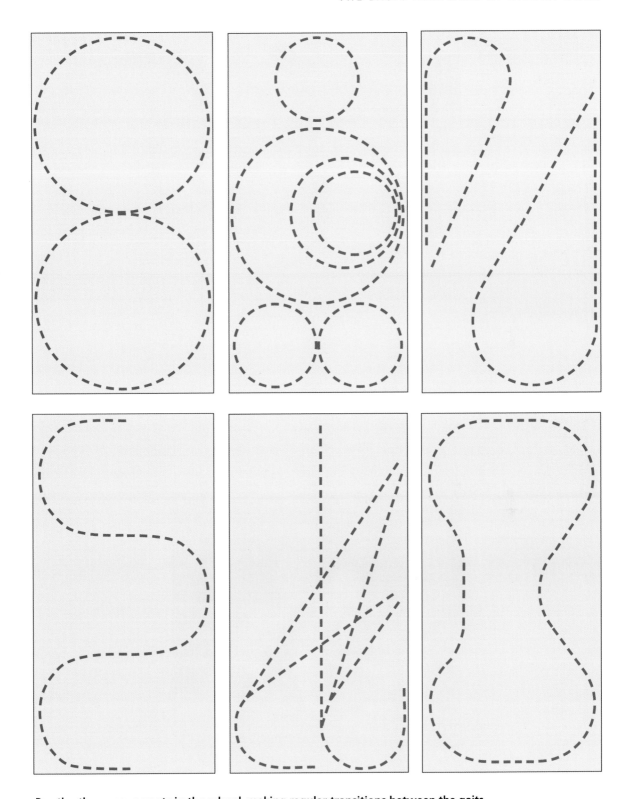

Practise these movements in the school, making regular transitions between the gaits.

Billy showing the unshakeable foundation that is inside bend on a circle in trot, here on a small circle.

the required direction. As before, if your cob does not respond to the leg, tap your boot a few times with your whip, but try not to let him go forward too much by catching his forwardness in the outside rein and through your body.

When making the turns and riding circles, remember to ride with your inside hip forward so you are not tempted to turn with your hands. If, at any time, forwardness, flexion or responsiveness are lost, stop and go back a step in the training process. These circles and turns can

Here Billy and Mel are preparing for a 20m circle. Billy is showing the right amount of bend to achieve this circle successfully.

A valuable view from outside the circle, showing the stretch the cob needs to give on the outside. It also shows the rider's outside leg correctly positioned behind the girth (the little toe could be a little lower, to keep the toe from pointing out) and the rider framing her cob well.

be easily built into the other exercises we have worked on so far. The key is to keep things simple, make changes of rein often and ride many transitions in between all of these movements.

On the Bit Round

Once your cob can flex and relax his jaw, give inside and outside flexion, and give the correct bend while maintaining correct forwardness and energy, you can assume he is on the bit for his level of training. Being on the bit is not just the shape your cob makes with his head and neck; it is also about the balance he achieves with his body, the energy he generates with his hind legs and his respect for *all* your aids, including those on the outside from your outside rein and outside leg. When he is on the bit, he will be more inclined to listen to your seat aids and respond with greater ease. All of the exercises in this book are designed to develop and enhance this.

Billy round and on the bit because he is accepting Mel's contact rather than just because he is flexing to the inside. A lovely image of a pure diagonal trot from a supple cob.

Some Stretching

Another exercise that tests the success of the previous training is the stretch. Please understand that the quality of the stretch that your cob gives should be a testament to the quality of the training in a normal 'uphill' contact. Do not school just for the stretch, as the stretch itself will not develop correct bend, true suppleness or the correct contact. Concentrating on the stretch alone will put most horses on the forehand, none more so than our chunky cobs, and so if you work on the stretch alone, the other qualities we look for and are seeking so diligently to develop in a dressage cob are unlikely to develop. However, if you use the stretch as an assessment of the previous work it can be one of your most invaluable tools. All you need to do is keep a small flexion through your fingers as you lower your hands and allow the reins to slip quietly through your hands. When invited, your cob will take some of the rein length and extend his frame. He will only go to where he is comfortable. You can ask for a little more stretch with a little more flexion from the fingers, followed by a little more give with the hands. If he obliges, be aware that it is more difficult for him and do not keep the lower stretch too long. Be careful not to allow the rhythm of the gait to quicken; keep the change of bend and softness in the contact and use your body to support your cob. If not ridden properly many cobs will plop onto their forehands.

Free walk on a long rein should be practised in each schooling session from your cob's earliest education. Stretching in the trot can be started as soon as your cob can relax his jaw and maintain a rounded outline, for a couple of seconds initially, and developed from there. Once your cob has developed collection in the canter using counter-canter and canter shoulder-in, stretching can be started in the canter.

THE PHOTO SEQUENCE OPPOSITE

ABOVE LEFT Billy showing the preferred horizontal stretch in trot without loss of balance. Any lower and you would risk putting your cob on the forehand.

BELOW LEFT Free walk with a natural neck. A lower stretch as shown by Billy would be ideal for stretching work, but this is perfect for relaxation, warming up or cooling down.

ABOVE RIGHT Ketchup showing a deeper stretch, again without losing balance. This is not ideal for most cobs as they can easily tighten their neck muscles and put themselves on their forehand.

BELOW RIGHT Ketchup reaching forward with her mouth to find the contact. She has a lower, longer stretch of her neck than she did in the previous image. It seems, however, that I am trying to 'sort out my knitting'.

CHAPTER THIRTEEN

Engaging Lateral Steps and Shoulder-In

First Steps of Lateral Work

Once you have developed a more sophisticated way of going through the use of transitions, softening of the jaw, bend and the use of school movements, and assuming that your cob can maintain balance, rhythm and energy throughout these movements and transitions on both reins, you are ready to move on to early lateral work through the laterally engaging steps of leg-yielding and shoulder-in. If you have followed the in-hand work to this level, you'll be suitably impressed with how easy your cob will now find his work!

PREREQUISITES

As we have worked through these exercises in-hand, we already know what these movements are and what benefits they offer you and your cob. Here we are looking simply at how to develop them in the ridden work and what the necessary prerequisites are in terms of both ridden work and in-hand work. We can summarize these prerequisites as follows:

Cob's Prerequisites In terms of ridden work, he must maintain softness and inside bend and flexion on both reins, on circles of varying sizes and through transitions from trot to walk, walk to halt and so on. From an in-hand point of view it is recommended that your cob can work through these exercises with ease as this ability will be used to build up the ridden work, with, initially, support from the ground.

Rider's Prerequisites Your posture and position must be close to correct, with an upright pelvis that does not tip to one side or the other. You should be able to feel the undulations of your cob's back so that you can apply the leg aids at the right moment without needing to look down.

Engaging Lateral Steps of Leg-Yield

SEQUENCE OF DEVELOPMENT

This should be developed in walk initially. Walk a circle about 10m in diameter in the middle of the arena. Slow the rhythm of the walk almost to halt. Maintain the bend and flexion to the inside and place your outside rein down towards the withers, while maintaining soft tension down towards the mouth on that side. When you are ready, use a unilateral leg aid with just your inside leg, in time with the swing of your cob's belly. If the timing is right, your outside hip will be lifted up and

Lucinda and Ted performing the lateral engaging steps of leg-yield. Because of his big Clydesdale frame, Ted will really benefit from the balance these steps will produce.

forward by your cob's back: allow this to be slightly exaggerated at the same moment as you check on the outside rein. This will prevent your cob from getting faster and from pushing onto his outside shoulder, and will help him to step to the outside of the circle. Try it for a couple of steps; as soon as you feel him step out to the outside, stop and reward him. If he does not step sideways, back up your leg aid with your whip, either behind your inside leg or on your boot, and check that he is not walking too fast. You can have assistance from the ground if he finds this difficult (*see* Chapter 6), while you ride through these engaging steps. Remember to do this on both reins. Be mindful that, at least in the early stages, your cob will find it easier in one direction than the other. Over time these differences will lessen to a stage at which the leg-yield will become fairly even on each rein.

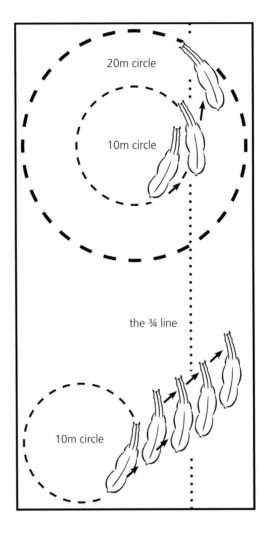

20m circle

10m circle

the ¾ line

10m circle

Developing leg-yielding.

Once he can step sideways for two or three steps from the circle, it is time to turn onto a straight line and step sideways towards the track. Start initially from the inner track. Work through this exercise gradually, giving your cob more and more room to step laterally. Once he is happy stepping out from the inner track, turn down the three-quarter line and finally ride from the centre line. Each time you change the exercise you may initially need help from someone on the ground. Do not be scared to have this help as it truly does stop any misunderstandings between you and your cob. Gradually, however, help from the ground should become superfluous. This help can thus be withdrawn as your cob becomes proficient, though occasional help on his stiffer side may still be necessary.

Once he is working smoothly through these laterally engaging steps on both reins in walk, you can try it in trot. Again, build up the exercise in exactly the same way, starting from an inner track and gradually moving out to the three-quarter line and then the centre line. If at any point your cob finds it difficult, go back a stage; try again at walk and see if you can diagnose what went wrong. Make sure the outside rein works against the cob's shoulder and that he does not swing his shoulders out too far while leaving his quarters behind.

Two consecutive steps of leg-yielding. Clear crossing is seen here in trot, with clear bend away from the direction of movement. Although there is clear bend, it is even throughout the cob's body and balance is maintained. If the bend produced is just neck bend, the balance will be very much on the shoulders.

Sometimes cobs, especially older ones who have come to this kind of schooling later on in life, may find sideways movement just too much to think about. If that is the case, reverse the direction of the engaging steps. To do this, working on the track, begin to ask your cob to give you outside flexion. When passing the A or C marker, cut off the next corner and head a little way down the track on the next long side. This helps to establish positioning to the outside. Upon reaching the track, keep outside flexion, keep the steps slow and use your outside leg to push your cob's body towards the inside of the school. Leg-yielding in this way gives you a visual boundary and, by riding with outside flexion into this boundary, you may find your cob is a little more accepting of sideways movement. This movement is rather like the counter shoulder-in in angle and can also be used to develop the counter shoulder-in later on.

Shoulder-In

SEQUENCE OF DEVELOPMENT

Once your engaging steps of leg-yielding are progressing well on both reins and your cob's sideways steps are deliberate, controlled and even, you can begin to build up to shoulder-in. In my experience people do not build up to the shoulder-in progressively enough or put the foundation stones in place, but rush through the teaching of this movement, expecting things just to happen. They then get into difficulty and start to create problems that should not have been there in the first place. It should not be like that at all and, with the foundation stones well laid, education in shoulder-in can be swift.

Now that your cob is proficient at the engaging steps, it is time to take him to the track on his 'easy' rein. Having used that term, I should emphasize that, first of all, you need to feel that you have your cob fairly even on both reins. Some people use far too much inside rein in a misguided attempt to create angle, while just as many use far too much outside rein and, as a result, inhibit any inclination of their cob to give correct bend. So, once you have your cob working evenly into both reins, ask for a *little* flexion to the inside – only enough to see the corner of your cob's eye/nostril. Maintain this inside flexion and support it with your inside leg, in time with the swing of his belly.

A lovely picture of Mel and Billy in shoulder-in.

Hopefully, you should soon feel your cob giving inside bend easily and this is the point at which you can start to build an angle.

To build angle into your cob's shoulder-in, ride through the second corner on your short side maintaining the aiding just explained, then turn your upper body to the inside so that your shoulders frame the angle of the shoulder-in. Keeping an even contact, you can now just give a little tickle down the outside rein with your outside hand low and close in to your cob's withers. Tickle at the same time as you put your inside leg on. This will stop your cob's outside foreleg from pushing back to the fence, or him escaping onto that outside shoulder.

The angle of the shoulder-in is much smaller than people think. So initially, keep the angle small and build it up gradually. Start with just one or two steps before releasing your cob forward into a freer medium walk and reward him for a good effort. Gradually ask for a few more steps but do not expect too much; the more transitions you do into and out of shoulder-in, the quicker it will become established in your cob's repertoire.

RIGHT The moment of coming through the corner, building the bend for shoulder-in in the next stride. Here Ketchup is at a shoulder-fore angle. There is a slight tilt of her head, probably because I've been too restrictive with my outside rein.

If you feel that you are not getting *any* angle in your shoulder-in, it may be worth trying to free your cob's shoulders to the inside by taking a step across the arena with his shoulders, rather like the first step across the diagonal when changing the rein. Then, the sequence is the same. Often, riders on cobs that tend to do this have too much inside rein and not enough outside rein, so making sure the reins feel even as you free your cob's shoulder to the inside will really help.

If your cob tends to give a big angle, but you feel he does not really give enough bend, go back a stage and ride the bend and flexion on the straight first. Only once increased flexion and bend are given should you open your shoulders to the inside slightly. This is generally a rider's error and a result of trying too hard. So, if it happens to you, think about riding a tiny angle and keeping it under control – do not get carried away!

Shoulder-in should, of course, be practised on both reins and, once established in walk, should be perfected in trot. All of the requirements are the same; remember your inside leg works with the swing of the cob's belly as the inside hind leg swings forward.

Again, if your cob finds this work difficult in trot and you have developed engaging steps of leg-yield in an outside bend, then you may

RIGHT A three-track shoulder-in in walk.

FAR RIGHT And here in trot, with the diagonal pair of left foreleg and right hind leg clearly working together on the same track.

need to practise counter shoulder-in. In the beginning, the counter shoulder-in is easier for your cob. The steps are exactly the same, except, if you practise counter shoulder-in, you should avoid getting too close to the fence!

I find that the shoulder-in is the turning point in many cobs' education. It is the point where the rider really feels their cob come off his shoulders, making him more manoeuvrable and even lighter and suppler than he was before. I think that this is the point at which cob and rider can really start to 'dance together', reading one another almost telepathically.

FAR LEFT A rear view of Vicky and Sound Barrier in a finished shoulder-in.

LEFT A view from diagonally across the arena showing a clearly framed rider with no tilts, twists or shoves with the seat.

CHAPTER FOURTEEN

Travers, Renvers and Half-Pass

Riding Specific Lateral Exercises

So, to this point, you have developed a forward, rhythmical, supple cob that will go sideways as easily as he goes forward. You and he are starting to mirror one another and most of the movements such as circles, loops and serpentines are becoming easy to ride. I believe the point at which you start to school the travers, renvers and half-pass is the transition between more elementary work and the work of finesse. Congratulations; once you have reached this point, you have reached a true milestone.

PREREQUISITES

I have, in effect, made reference to the prerequisites for this work in my opening sentences of this chapter, but they can be further summarized as follows:

Cob's Prerequisites In terms of ridden work, he must maintain softness and inside bend and flexion on both reins, on circles of varying sizes and through transitions from trot to walk, walk to halt and so on. Your cob should understand the previous leg-yielding exercise with inside bend as well as the exercise in outside bend, and he should be able to perform shoulder-in and counter shoulder-in in walk and trot. From an in-hand point of view, it is recommended that your cob can work through all three of these exercises with ease, as this ability will be used to build up the ridden work, initially with support from the ground.

Rider's Prerequisites Your posture and position must be close to correct, with an upright pelvis that does not tip to one side or the other. You should be able to feel the undulations of your cob's back so that you can apply the leg aid at the right moment without needing to look down.

Travers

SEQUENCE OF DEVELOPMENT

This should be developed in walk initially. There are a couple of ways to develop travers on your cob, but I find the following to be the easiest. Walk a circle about 10m diameter in one of the corners of the arena which leads onto the long side. Slow the rhythm of the walk almost to halt. Maintain the bend and flexion to the inside and place your outside rein down towards the withers, while maintaining soft tension

Sound Barrier showing travers in trot.

down towards the cob's mouth on that side. On the circle, use a uni-lateral leg aid with your inside leg in time with the swing of your cob's belly to develop bend while on the circle. As you come round past the corner of the arena, allow your inside leg to slip forward (keep it close to your cob so he stays in the correct bend) as you advance your inside hip a little more. As your cob reaches the track with his fore feet, fix the angle of your body to the outside. Slip your outside leg back and use it with the swing of the cob's belly. Keep your eyes looking down the track and initially avoid riding for too much angle. Keep your inside leg close so you can correct your cob if he tries to change his bend to the outside. Raise your inside hand, keeping your cob flexed to the inside but keep the feeling down both reins fairly even. Keep the walk slow and, after three or four steps, stop and reward.

Generally speaking, at this stage the angle of the movement is not a problem as your cob has already become proficient at stepping sideways. What he may find difficult is maintaining his bend into the direction of the movement as, up until now, his bend has always been away from the movement. So, to help this, ride your inside bend fairly strongly into the travers and keep your inside rein raised a little, asking

This image shows how I have fixed the angle with my shoulders.

for him to flex a little more to the inside. Once the angle is established off the outside leg, the inside leg, brushed forward, can work a little more to help with the bend. Increase the number of strides your cob can achieve until he is able to maintain a full long side of travers on both reins.

PHOTO SEQUENCE ABOVE
Consecutive steps of travers in walk. The angle is maintained with squared shoulders with the rider looking towards the outside of the arena.

Another way to establish travers would be to ride into shoulder-in, then change your body from being positioned to the inside to being positioned to the outside, while increasing the pressure from the outside leg to bring your cob's quarters in. Using this method introduces more torque into your cob's body, increasing the bend to the inside. It is therefore an exercise that would be worthwhile trying once travers has been established by the method just described, in order to increase difficulty.

Once travers is established in walk, travers in trot should be built up step by step. As with the shoulder-in, the development of trot travers should follow the development for walk. Keep the trot slow and just remember to use the outside leg with the swing of the cob's belly.

Once the basics of travers are established, you can begin to concentrate on increasing bend to the inside. To do this, your inside leg becomes much more important. Your shoulders, framing the movement,

Travers in trot. Front view.   Travers in trot. Rear view.

maintain the angle, and now with your inside leg slipped forward, you use it to increase bend and feel as though you are using it to push your cob into your outside rein. This will increase bend and, coupled with the exercise just mentioned of riding from shoulder-in to travers, will give you full control over your cob's lateral suppleness.

The final development would be to reverse the above-mentioned exercise to riding from travers to shoulder-in. Again, the key to a successful transition is through your body angle. So, to go from travers to shoulder-in, you must change from the travers position, through to straight (default position) and then develop the shoulder-in from there. Initially the transition can be slow, but soon the transition can be made within a few strides. As with everything else so far, this should be practised on both reins and, once established in walk, should be developed in trot.

Walk Pirouette

This is the point at which I teach the walk pirouette as an extension of travers. It is taught on a circle about 5–10m in diameter. Once on the circle, ride travers around the circle. Do not stay in this position for too long: no more than half a circle at a time. Gradually the travers circle can be made smaller, a metre at a time. Do not go too small too quickly as your cob will find it too difficult and will stiffen and stop moving his inside hind leg. Over weeks, you can gradually bring the circle down to about 5m diameter while maintaining the travers position. You are now in a large working pirouette. Keep inside flexion throughout but do not exaggerate it. For the time being, large working pirouettes are enough. Later on, to produce a true pirouette, it will be necessary to make the figure smaller, but do not practise this too soon or too often as you want to keep your cob's hindleg stepping. Practising mainly in larger working pirouettes will help to avoid errors.

Half-Pass

SEQUENCE OF DEVELOPMENT

I teach half-pass once travers is established. In many ways it is a similar exercise except that the line along which your cob will be travelling is a diagonal one. If shoulder-in and travers have been well understood by your cob, half-pass will come easily.

Start your cob's half-pass education in walk and begin teaching it from the centre line. Start on the rein on which your cob finds the

FAR LEFT Front view of Sound Barrier and Vicky in trot half-pass.

LEFT Billy and Mel also showing a lovely half-pass.

Walk half-pass from the centre line. Hayley has Danny clearly flexed into the direction of the movement.

travers easier. Turn down the centre line and, from the turn, keep your inside hip pushed a little forward; allow this to deepen your leg and remember, as with travers, to keep your inside leg close to your cob's barrel. Keep your shoulders facing straight ahead and do not twist either way. Your inside hand is raised to help keep your cob flexed to the inside and your outside hand is kept lower by your cob's withers. The outside rein is used to help nudge the outside shoulder over. Your outside leg then slips back behind the girth and is used in time with the swing of your cob's belly at the same time as your inside hip advances up and forward. Your eyes look towards where you want your cob to go. After a couple of sideways steps, praise your cob, stop the exercise and let him walk free. At the moment it is important not to make the angle steep. Build up these half-pass steps a couple at a time. Use a full long side to get back to the track in walk.

Once this work is becoming established on both reins, you can vary your starting position. For example, rather than starting down the centre line, after travelling through a corner on the outside track, start the half-pass at one of the quarter markers (K, H, M or F) or even at the halfway markers E or B. Also consider starting from a shoulder-in position as this will help bend and articulation of the shoulder and increase collection. The transition is rather similar to what we have already discussed for shoulder-in to travers. Establish the shoulder-in and, as you switch, change your body first (fairly quickly) and then apply your half-pass aids. At first the transition from shoulder-in to half-pass may be slow but soon, and with practice, your cob should be able to make a clean transition from shoulder-in to half-pass within a stride or two. Later on, once your cob has the idea, you could also ride half-pass from travers. With this, however, be careful not to allow the quarters to lead once in the half-pass. To ride half-pass from travers, ride the travers through the short side of the arena then, as you come round the corner, keep turning your cob (as though about to change the rein) until his shoulders lead the quarters and then ride half-pass across the arena. These exercises need to be practised on both reins and in both walk and trot.

ABOVE Once proficient in walk, trot half-pass can be developed.

Half-pass in trot. The forehand clearly leads the quarters.

Again showing the forehand clearly leading the quarters.

If problems arise, go back a step and think about the basics. If your cob tries to lead with his quarters in half-pass, make all your transitions to half-pass from shoulder-in and try riding no more than four strides of half-pass before riding the shoulder-in again. If your cob stops going forward through this, make the half-pass angle less steep. If your cob lacks bend in half-pass, return to the shoulder-in to travers transitions and make repeated transitions between the two before reattempting a half-pass and try to maintain the influence of that exercise in your half-passes.

An alternative view of trot half-pass from the outside of the bend. It shows the stretch your cob needs to give while crossing the foreleg and maintaining the necessary bend.

Renvers

SEQUENCE OF DEVELOPMENT

Renvers is a movement I very rarely ride, to be honest. I rarely 'school' it but I do occasionally ride it purely as a test of my influence over all parts of the cob I am riding. It lets me know whether I can control my cob's shoulders through the influence of the shoulder-in, and it also lets me know whether I can control my cob's quarters using the skills of riding the travers, and it confirms my ability to ride an accurate bend.

Although it is really an identical exercise to travers (the only change is the side on which the wall is in relation to the bend), it is a very good diagnostic movement in a way that travers is not. It is also ridden and developed very differently as a result of the need for a change of bend to a counter-flexion.

I ride renvers from the half-pass. To do this exercise your cob will need to be able to half-pass at a fairly steep angle so that, if starting at either D or G on the centre line in a 20 × 40m arena, he is back at the track just after the halfway markers of B or E. (If you have the luxury of a 60m arena your half-passes need not be quite so steep.) I half-pass from the centre line towards the track, arriving just after the halfway marker. Just before I get there I slow the steps and I begin to use my body much in

the same way as I described for the shoulder-in to travers transition by pivoting my body and shoulder position from facing straight ahead to facing the middle of the arena, rather like the shoulder-in position but, of course, maintaining the bend set up in the half-pass and therefore the opposite bend to the shoulder-in.

Ketchup in renvers on an inner track.

The aim is to prevent the cob's shoulders from advancing while pushing the quarters over to the track. This is done without changing bend at all. Once the renvers position is established, with the cob in counter-flexion, quarters out and shoulders in, the steps should be easy, as all you are doing is a version of travers. The difficulty is the transition and positioning of your cob for the first few steps. Again, this should be done in walk initially and, once your cob is enjoying some success with this, you can build up to the trot. Expect just a couple of steps at a time initially and remember the all-important reward once he has achieved this.

Renvers can also be established from shoulder-in. To do this, establish the shoulder-in in walk. Once established, increase the angle of the shoulder-in by opening your shoulders a little more to the inside. At this point your leg position changes, from inside leg being forward at the girth to being back behind the girth, and outside leg from behind

From the half-pass, I am pushing the quarters over, and slowing Ketchup's shoulders down so that when we reach the inner track we can continue down the track in renvers.

the girth to at the girth, and the action of your hands changes, lowering the inside hand towards the withers and raising the outside hand. This helps to change the bend and flexion of the shoulder-in to create the renvers. Maintain the angle while changing your cob's bend from the shoulder-in bend to the inside of the arena, to the renvers bend to the outside of the arena. (Therefore, if you are on the right rein, you will be changing from right bend in the shoulder-in (right leg acting for right bend at the girth with the right rein flexing to the inside) to left bend (where your left leg acts forward at the girth for bend, your left rein flexing your cob to the outside of the arena, while your right leg swings back to keep the quarters on the track and the right rein supports the action of the right leg and supports the shoulders.)

Renvers in walk can also be achieved after a walk pirouette ridden out on the track. After two-thirds of the pirouette, slow the travel of the shoulders. Achieve your renvers body position, and then 'scoop' the renvers along the track. These exercises should be increasingly easy as you progress because your cob should be more and more responsive and much more supple than he was before.

....

CHAPTER FIFTEEN

Rein-Back

The Role of the Ridden Rein-Back

The exercises mentioned so far have developed lateral suppleness and have started to develop collection through flexing and mobilizing the hind leg joint system. The rein-back develops this collecting ability but in a different way. In particular, the rein-back develops much more the pelvic tilt, which positions your cob's pelvis at a greater angle, dropping the rear end of the pelvis while coiling his loins and lifting his back. The rein-back is well known for getting all horses 'back onto their hocks' and, when practised within the choreography of school exercises discussed so far, brings about a much more advanced way of going.

PREREQUISITES

The introduction of the rein-back in-hand was discussed in Chapter 4. Additional to this, in terms of introducing it under saddle, the prerequisites can be summarized as follows:

Cob's Prerequisites He must maintain softness and inside bend and flexion on both reins on circles of varying sizes and through transitions from trot to walk, walk to halt and so on. He can begin to work through rein-back at the same time that he starts working on the leg-yielding exercises and other lateral movements.

Rider's Prerequisites Your posture and position must be close to correct, with an upright pelvis that does not tip to one side or the other. You should be able to maintain a steady, correct contact without pulling back or dropping the contact and therefore 'deserting' the cob.

SEQUENCE OF DEVELOPMENT

Because you have worked through rein-back in-hand, this should not pose too much of a problem for your cob to pick up. Do not do anything to make it hard either; keep it simple. When things are kept simple, understanding can be achieved fairly quickly. To start with, in walk, carry out the following checklist. Check your position, especially of your pelvis and legs. Then check your contact, making sure you have

RIGHT The halt before the rein-back. I have moved my legs back to aid for the rein-back, though they would not normally need to go this far back. (Actually, the reason for my leg position in the photos in this chapter is that, when they were taken, Ketchup was pregnant and we had a bit of a belly to accommodate. This may also give the illusion that the saddle was positioned rather forward although, in fact, the placement was correct.)

BELOW LEFT Here Ketchup shifts her weight back and starts her first step in the rein-back. She has also softened the contact.

BELOW RIGHT The second step.

an even, light contact down each rein. Make sure your reins are short enough to carry out the following exercise (*see* below). Now is your preparation time as, when you are in the middle of the movement, pauses can cause confusion in your cob.

Once you have completed your checklist, bring your cob to a halt. Quickly make another check of the points above. Now, take your time on the next few points. First of all, check your contact. Your cob will try to walk on when you place your legs on him, so make sure you will be able to 'catch' that forward impetus and divert the energy into backward steps. Then fold your shoulders forward slightly, making sure you fold from the hips without rounding your back. Allow your lower legs to slip back a few centimetres while deepening your thigh position down and back. Once in this position, close both of your legs together. You should feel a 'forward' impulse through your cob and it is at this moment that you need to catch it and stop it going forward. While we *never* pull our cobs back into the rein-back, the hand must stop that forward tendency. Your cob should know the word 'back' from your in-hand work, so use it now and, if need be, ask a helper to work your cob in the way that you developed the rein-back dismounted. This should negate the inclination to get stronger and stronger with your hands and will eliminate the tendency to pull your cob back with the hands.

Once he has taken one step, reward him as we always do for a correct reaction. When he knows what you want he will give it more easily and will find it easier to give you more and more steps. However, do not ask for too many steps initially and be quick to release the movement into forward motion again by allowing a little more with your contact, releasing your hands forward, sitting back up into your normal riding position and releasing your leg pressure while returning your legs back to their normal neutral position. Your cob will feel the difference and will step forward out of the rein-back. Build up from two or three steps to a maximum of about five or six initially. (Personally, I rarely ride more than five or six steps but, if you intend to do so, you should work towards this gradually – as ever when schooling a movement, it is quality, not quantity, that matters.)

Once you can get a few steps of rein-back you can begin to modify the steps. First, you may well notice that your cob steps sideways with his quarters. To counteract this you can flex him into the same direction that his quarters want to push. At the same time, keep the other rein close to his shoulder so you effectively keep his shoulders over into the direction his quarters want to go, and this should stop the quarters from swinging. Another problem could be that your cob comes very low with his head during the rein-back steps. If this happens, a higher hand-carriage will help to keep his poll up but it is essential to apply this aiding carefully. Too strong a contact could drop your cob's poll and place him on his shoulders, and too much upward pressure could hollow him and drop his sternum, both of which would

CLOCKWISE FROM TOP LEFT This rein-back sequence shows a more advanced looking rein-back with a better contact, and much better 'sitting' behind. This is partly because of straightness, but also because of the repeated transitions into and out of the rein-back, initially from walk, and later from trot.

be the antithesis of what is required. Other cobs may become hollow in their first attempts at rein-back. For these cobs, you will need to keep a flexing, tickling contact, to keep him soft in your hands.

Once your rein-back is coming along nicely, repeated walk, rein-back, walk transitions can take place. Later, trot, halt, rein-back, trot transitions can be attempted and of course these should be interjected with any and all of the lateral movements that your cob learns. Only in this way will each exercise fully realize its potential for modifying your cob's way of going and maximizing his muscular development.

....

CHAPTER SIXTEEN

Developing Canter

Why Canter is Introduced Quite Late

I have left canter until fairly late in the exercises and this is for a good reason. Generally speaking, it is because the balance for the canter must be developed through other movements; it cannot be developed purely by riding the canter. Your cob needs to develop a more sophisticated way of going in walk and trot first, because most cobs are built to load their forehands easily and the rock in the canter accentuates this tendency. Therefore, until your cob can lift up through his shoulders, the canter will inevitably be on the forehand and thus unbalanced. However, with his way of going modified, the first attempts at canter can be much more 'uphill' and impulsive and this avoids the all-too-common tug of war that arises when a rider tries to 'pull' the cob into balance.

PREREQUISITES

The prerequisites for developing canter are:

Cob's Prerequisites In terms of ridden work, he must maintain softness and inside bend and flexion on both reins on circles of varying sizes and through transitions from trot to walk, walk to halt and so on. He should be forward and energetic off the leg through all transitions. He should at least be able to perform the leg-yielding exercises as well as rein-back.

Rider's Prerequisites Your posture and position must be close to correct, with an upright pelvis that does not tip to one side or the other. You should be able to maintain a steady, correct contact without pulling back or dropping the contact and therefore 'deserting' your cob.

SEQUENCE OF DEVELOPMENT

Initially, we shall work on the transition; this is where the quality of the canter is determined. If your cob is allowed to run into the canter the gait will inevitably be heavy on the forehand and your cob will feel out of control. Try the first few transitions out of trot. On a circle of about 20m diameter, get your canter aids organized: inside hip pushing forward, inside leg on the girth, outside leg by virtue of this placed back from the hip. The outside leg does nothing more than indicate which canter lead you require; it is the inside leg that requests the transition. If you apply the canter aids and your cob either does nothing or runs a little in the trot, re-establish the correct trot and this time prepare him a little more – tap your boot with your whip, or give him a tickle behind your leg a stride or two before you ask for canter again. As the main aid for canter is your inside leg, if you do need to tap your cob, or your boot, I would recommend doing so to the inside, so you

The moment of the transition. A little hollow, and I suspect that the cob was not quite off Lucinda's legs.

support your main aid. I always want to make things as clear as possible to the cobs I ride so, if one leg needs reinforcing, I make sure that I use the whip on the same side. As soon as he strikes off, take your weight forward over your thighs and give him a great big pat. You may need to sharpen him up before the transition and then again through the trans-ition to get it. Consistency at this point pays off in the end.

As with all the exercises, this must be done on both reins and, as with everything else we have discussed so far, your cob will initially find one rein much easier than the other. It is the gymnastic effects of the exer-cises described in this book that will help to even out those differences. While you must school on both reins in the canter itself, the ease with which the canter develops is often closely related to the lateral work, particularly if this is developed thoroughly in walk.

Soon, you should be able to make repeated trot-canter-trot transitions, keeping each gait for half a 20m circle at a time. In the canter, keep a slightly forward seat and, once into the trot, bring the rhythm back to a controllable level. Always take your time over the upward transitions, making sure your aiding is very exact so that your cob is never unsure of what you are asking.

At this stage do not worry about the quality of your cob's downward transition to trot. Pay more attention to the quality of your riding in the transition. In the main, you need to ride the transition with your body and your seat, not your hands. All your hands do is maintain the softness, giving little flexions whenever your cob feels stiff or resistant in his mouth, or when he tries to lift his head too high, or push into your hands. For the transition, your body balances a little behind the movement, giving a little resistance to the forward canter steps and encouraging the canter rhythm to slow. Your gluteal muscles and inner thighs (the active parts of your seat in this context) close, initially in the rhythm of the canter, to slow it, and then in a more sustained way as the transition is imminent. These aids can be maintained for a stride

Mel and Billy showing a soft, round canter transition on a 20m circle.

or two in trot after the transition has been successful, until the trot is at the correct speed and rhythm.

Once this exercise is becoming established, you can begin to work through walk to canter exercises. The aiding remains the same and works well after a couple of canter transitions from trot. Take walk for two or three strides and then ask for canter. As long as your cob has been thinking 'forward' during your previous transitions, the canter should not be too hard to obtain from walk. If you do find it more difficult, repeated transitions from walk via trot will help. Initially, count four strides of trot before asking for canter. When this is successful, the transition can be requested after three strides and finally after two or one. (Perhaps because they think the walk to canter transition requires a good deal of 'speeding up', some riders tend to 'ask' too strongly for this transition, but this is not the key. If you resort to stronger aids, you will end up with a cob whose reactions to the leg are duller. If necessary, you can use the above-mentioned technique of your whip tapping your inside boot just before the transitions, so your cob is aware of what is coming and that he needs to give you energy in the transition from the gentlest of aids.)

Initially, the canter should be ridden in a slightly forward seat, but once the walk to canter transition is established, a fuller, more upright

Midge and Jane showing what frequent transitions can achieve. Look at the engagement of that near hind leg!

seat should be taken. At this point you should start to ask for a little more bend in the canter and this is where, coupled with the dynamic effect of the walk to canter transition, the canter should start to 'jump', bascule and lighten off the shoulders. Reward any glimpses of a more 'uphill' canter so your cob knows what kind of canter you want.

Soon you should be starting to vary the size of the canter circles, varying the places where you ask for a canter strike-off from walk, and you can even intersperse canter work with walk shoulder-in, which will help make the canter much more advanced in its form. As mentioned earlier, it is often the development of movements such as shoulder-in in walk that improve the quality of the canter, but it is also useful to develop transitions to canter out of walk shoulder-in, particularly if your cob has a 'tricky' lead. By positioning your cob in shoulder-in, you are placing him in the most beneficial position to pick up canter successfully. This is usually because the cob can no longer dive out through one of his shoulders (quite often in the outside shoulder-in canter transitions).

It is at this point that you can begin to 'work' the downward transitions from the canter to a balanced trot. Making sure that the canter has sufficient bend, and that your cob is accepting a light, round contact, you can begin to collect the canter for a few strides before you ask your cob to come down to trot. To collect him, use your seat muscles, especially at the lowest part of the canter stride, closing these muscles at the same time as pulsing with your lower leg (usually your inside leg will suffice, but sometimes if you are needing more response, both legs together) in order to produce a shorter canter stride before you ride forward to trot. The trot transition should then feel as if your cob steps up to a rhythmical, even trot without falling forward, rushing or getting strong in the hands.

This image shows the value of walk to canter transitions and shoulder-in in canter. Look at how this 'uphill' stride is developing.

Once you can feel your cob collect for those few strides before the transition to trot, you can take your canter down the long side and ask for a stride or two of canter shoulder-in. Collect the canter as above and, as you come round the corner onto the long side, increase the inside leg aid and then turn your shoulders to the inside. Keep this up for two strides and then release, taking the weight onto your thighs and going into a forward seat to reward your cob. Make sure you do this on both reins – though do not be surprised if it is initially much easier on one rein than the other, and that his more difficult rein takes much longer to establish.

Once the canter is established, a give and re-take of the reins will test self-carriage. Billy is clearly showing he can keep his own balance.

Counter-Canter

Once the work above is established, counter-canter can soon be attempted. The key with counter-canter is not to make your cob bend over-much in one direction or the other, and always to think of ways of making it easy for him. Where you can, make the movements slow, and make the curves easy by keeping them shallow, cutting out corners and so on.

Start with easy shallow loops on the long side. Always keep an eye on the quality of the canter because if it deteriorates counter-canter will be impossible. When riding a shallow loop, initially start with one just a metre or two in from the track on the long side. The first part of the loop is easy, gradually bringing your cob in from the track. The next part is more difficult and your riding needs to be more delicate. Keeping your legs in the canter position, allow your shoulders to bring your cob back towards the track. At this point make sure that a slight inside bend (over the leading leg) is maintained and keep the return fairly gradual. Soon the loops can be made bigger, to 3m. When your cob can maintain a more collected feeling through the use of a few strides of canter shoulder-in, a 5m loop should not cause too much difficulty.

The next step will be to change the rein from a small (10–12m) circle, or a turn down the three-quarter line/centre line, returning to the track part of the way down the long side. To make it easier at first, once you have taken the diagonal line towards the track, you could start the turn into the counter-canter before actually reaching the track, making the line you follow more acute. This means that the turn into the counter-canter will be more gradual. Your cob will canter the straight line on the diagonal, then turn gradually from the diagonal line into the counter-canter at the track so that the angle is less severe once you reach the fence. The counter-canter should then be maintained only for a stride or two before returning to trot before the first corner. As before, the bend should be kept over the leading leg, your legs should maintain the canter position for the canter lead that you are riding and the canter should be kept contained.

Soon you should be able to keep the counter-canter through the first corner while maintaining the quality of the movement. This should be built upon over time, step by step, until you can ride a full half-circle of counter-canter before changing the rein again.

Canter Half-Pass

Once your cob is capable of canter shoulder-in and counter-canter on both reins, half-pass should be started. In a sense it is easier to start this movement in canter than in the other gaits because the canter stride has a natural 'rock', which can lead it into the direction of the half-pass. The aids, too, are a continuation of the canter aid, except that the rider's outside leg becomes more dominant. Timing is the key.

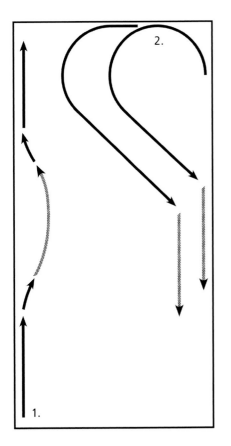

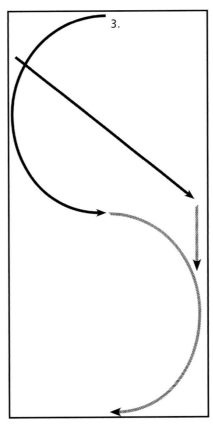

Exercises to develop counter-canter.

1. Start with a shallow loop on the long side, which can gradually be made a little deeper.

2. Proceed to turning a 15m half-circle, and riding just a couple of counter-canter strides as you return to the track.

3. Proceed to turning a 12–10m half-circle and riding a few more counter-canter strides as you return to the track.

Jane showing the engagement necessary for canter half-pass.

Apply the aid for the half-pass once in every canter stride, generally speaking at the low point of the stride just before your cob jumps up into the next stride. Build upon this step by step, in exactly the same way as when developing it in trot (*see* Chapter 14). Ride the canter half-pass in the same places as the trot, but return to trot at the end so you avoid the added complication of riding counter-canter straight afterwards. Pulse your legs for the sideways aid, but do not allow this to push your upper body off the default upright position.

To add to your control over your cob's canter, you can now begin to ride a set number of half-pass strides followed by a set number of canter shoulder-in strides. Initially, perhaps simply do about half the exercise in half-pass and half in shoulder-in. Soon, however, you should think about counting say three or four strides in half-pass followed by the same number in shoulder-in, and so on. This focus on precision gives real control over the bend in the half-pass and helps you to control exactly where your cob returns to the track after his diagonal line.

Over time, the extent to which your cob will jump sideways will increase until he will be able to turn past the centre line and still reach the track at the quarter marker after a canter half-pass. When he can do this while maintaining the quality of the canter, you can start to use the influence of the half-pass on the circle to build up to a working canter pirouette.

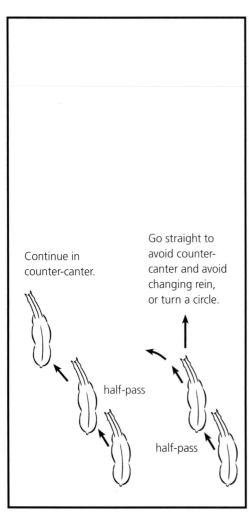

Continue in counter-canter.

Go straight to avoid counter-canter and avoid changing rein, or turn a circle.

half-pass

half-pass

Canter half-pass exercises.

CHAPTER SEVENTEEN

Lengthening the Trot and Canter

The Need to be Judicious

The extended and medium variations of the gaits are probably the most difficult for the cob. This is a consequence of their conformation being much more 'on the shoulders' than breeds such as Warmbloods, as well as the shorter, rounder nature of their movement. However, the key to their lengthened gaits is the quality of the collection that should be being built up while working on the transitions and the lateral movements. Further to this, I have left this chapter to near the end of the book, because I often find that it is developing the piaffe and, more significantly, the passage that really helps our cobs to establish their medium and extended gaits. So, work on true medium and extended trot, in particular, is often best left until you are working on these much more advanced collected movements. Lengthening the canter can, however, be started earlier, so once some early collected canter and counter-canter can be achieved, your cob may be ready to start work on the medium canter. Opening up the gait is slightly different from true lengthening and just ensures that your cob is still thinking forward. You can do this occasionally in the trot by putting your leg on and expecting your cob to 'take you' forward for up to five or six strides.

A trot that is clearly lengthening towards extension.

However, this is just a variation of rhythm, not true lengthening or a real precursor to the medium strides – it is more a check that you can vary the trot rhythm at will.

Before lengthening can be attempted, qualities such as rhythm, good bend, actively engaged hindquarters and an accepting contact – here demonstrated by a Clydesdale – must be established.

PREREQUISITES

As explained in the introductory sentences to this chapter, the pre-requisites for true medium and extended work relate closely to the earlier exercises that have contributed towards collection, and can be summarized as follows:

Cob's Prerequisites Your cob should at least be capable of shoulder-in in walk and trot, as well as transitions between the gaits, including the rein-back. He should be well connected to the bit, and easily allow his energy to travel from his hindquarters towards his mouth. For extension in canter, he should be able to make a balanced transition from canter to trot, and be capable of showing some collection through canter shoulder-in.

Rider's Prerequisites Your posture and position must be close to correct, with an upright pelvis that does not tip to one side or the other. You should be able to maintain a steady, correct contact without pulling back or dropping the contact and therefore 'deserting' your cob. As the medium and extended trot will be ridden in rising trot initially, the quality of your rising trot should be good.

Lengthening the Trot

SEQUENCE OF DEVELOPMENT

While there are not really exercises as such that develop this, there is a sequence that needs to be followed in its development. The asking and the aiding are the same throughout; the development comes through asking for more and more strides over time, and later on asking for greater length of stride when working towards extension rather than the medium gait.

In trot, really start to ride for collected trot strides – bubbly, energetic, slightly shorter ones – while maintaining a soft, even contact. It is from the truly collected trot that the medium, and later the extended, trot emerges. Once the trot is energetic and bubbly, close both legs, asking for a little more energy, and, as you start to rise to the lengthened strides, be ready to allow your hips to rock a little more forward towards the pommel of the saddle. Maintain the contact, making sure you do not throw the reins forward and allow the extra energy just to

Billy clearly lengthening his stride. A more 'uphill' frame will develop as his collection develops. Remember, extensions develop from good-quality collection.

gush out onto the forehand. Ask for one or two strides before making a true downward transition to return to your collected trot. Make sure you really ride the downward transition, as this will put your cob back onto his hocks and lighten the contact again.

If, when you ask for the lengthened strides, your cob does not respond to the leg aids, give him a tap behind the leg, or tap your boot, a couple of times before asking. This should have the desired effect. If, however, your cob rushes off, canters or runs onto his forehand, you will need to bring him back, re-establish the collected trot and make another attempt, this time asking for less but concentrating on keeping the rhythm slow while maintaining a positive contact.

The number of lengthened strides should be built up gradually; the main aim is to maintain harmony and rhythm, so only put in the amount of power that your cob can cope with without tipping onto his shoulders.

Lengthening the Canter

SEQUENCE OF DEVELOPMENT

Medium canter should be developed in pretty much the same way as the medium trot. Establish the collection in canter through repeated walk to canter transitions, ride some canter shoulder-in and then open up your cob's canter using repeated impulsive leg aids. When your cob goes forward, try not to let your shoulders rock back too much, as this will tip him onto his shoulders. Keep the contact even and steady. Maintain a longer canter stride for just two or three strides initially and then, as with the trot, ride a true transition to collected canter by closing your seat and inner thighs to sit your cob back onto his hocks.

If he has tipped onto his forehand, you may need to make a transition to trot and try again. Because canter is not the cob's most natural gait, tipping onto the forehand is much more likely during this exercise than in the trot. If this happens repeatedly, put in less power until you find how much your cob can take without falling onto his shoulders. Gradually, over time, power can be added without him losing his balance. This will happen mainly as a result of repeated transitions from collected to lengthened canter, but the work on canter shoulder-in, rein-back to canter transitions and the various lateral exercises in canter will all help to support the endeavour.

Early medium canter.

Medium canter.

A Word on Extensions

Full extensions in either trot or canter are rarely asked for of cobs because of their conformation and the physical effort required. This is especially so with the chunkier individuals, because it is so easy to tip the balance onto the forehand and sustained practice of this movement (especially if not of the best quality) could, in the long run, be damaging to the cob's joints. So please ride full extensions sparingly and always ride them progressively. When I do this, I ride a lot of medium strides in trot and canter. When those strides are feeling particularly balanced I will progressively open the cob up a little more. To do this I keep a more 'uphill' feeling through the contact, a gentle but raised hand, and lift my diaphragm, aiming the strides a little more 'uphill', with a feeling of support through the whole body I push for a bigger step. I would emphasize the warning not to force extension; ask only when your cob is really set up for it. If it is forced, unfortunately all the forced energy will end up on the forehand. Instead, set yourself and your cob up for success; stay positive and be patient – they can do it!

....

CHAPTER EIGHTEEN

Ridden Piaffe

Reaching the Pinnacle

Getting to this point is a real achievement. Well done! Piaffe is often seen as the hallmark of classical riding and certainly, by some, as the pinnacle of our sport. For a cob to get to this level is an even greater achievement.

PREREQUISITES

Piaffe is a prime example of a movement that only becomes possible once the foundations have been laid by correct, progressive work in other areas. The key prerequisites can be summarized as follows:

Cob's Prerequisites While it is essential that the basics of correct bend and way of going are established, it is not essential to have all the lateral exercises fully developed before beginning work on the ridden piaffe. It can, rather, be started alongside this lateral work. Much of the work towards piaffe is already happening within our transitions from rein-back anyway. Half-steps of piaffe should have become established in-hand as well. What must be remembered, however, is that the piaffe should, and indeed must, be developed slowly over months and years rather than days and weeks.

Rider's Prerequisites Your posture and position must be close to correct, with an upright pelvis that does not tip to one side or another. You should be able to maintain a steady, correct contact without pulling

The finished piaffe.

back or dropping the contact and therefore 'deserting' your cob. You should be well versed in the exercises of the rein-back and the correct aiding of that movement.

SEQUENCE OF DEVELOPMENT

As mentioned above, the piaffe work has already been started. The rein-back forms the foundation for the piaffe and, coupled with the transitions from rein-back into trot, the main method of bringing about this highly collected trot on the spot is already being consolidated. The key now is gradually, over weeks and months, to shorten the trot out of the rein-back. By doing this slowly, you maintain energy and lively impulsion while making the steps shorter and shorter. This is a long process that should not be rushed. Think about it as a system of conditioning your cob's muscles ready to perform a very difficult movement.

After some weeks of shortening the trot out of the rein-back, you will need to restrain as much forward impetus as possible out of the rein-back. Though piaffe must maintain a 'forward' feeling, you need to feel as though you have reduced the actual forward step to little more than 15cm per step – some riders indeed feel as though they have asked their cob to remain almost on the spot. This is done with your seat as well as your contact. At the moment of riding forwards out of the rein-back, your shoulders should come back to upright, but your lower legs

The rein-back, and its transitions to trot, are the basis for developing the piaffe.

need to stay back slightly, though not as far back as for the rein-back. As you restrain your cob's forward movement you will need to urge him to bounce up into a diagonalized rhythm. When you feel that first 'bounce' of the initial piaffe, stop and reward your cob and release him forward. Do not practise this too much in one session; rather build it up little and often.

Once he is diagonalizing easily for that initial bounce, ask for a few more steps, increasing just one step at a time. Keep your upper body feeling light and lofty as this will help get your cob up off his shoulders for the piaffe. When your cob diagonalizes his steps, maintain that 'forward' feeling as mentioned above, but keep the stride 'closed' so that each step remains about 15cm in length. This closed stride, while maintaining the forward attitude, keeps the strides developing towards a piaffe rather than leaking out towards a collected trot.

If your cob find this ridden progression too difficult, go back to in-hand work and use this as a basis for establishing the 'bounce' ridden. Either have someone helping from the ground, as described in Chapter 9, or alternatively use the whip in the way your cob recognizes from

Sound Barrier practising the half-steps of piaffe that come about as a result of the trot to rein-back to trot transitions.

the in-hand work in your ridden work. Again, build up slowly. One or two good steps are better than many incorrect or rushed ones.

In time, you can start to ask for the diagonalized steps from a shortened collected walk. To attain collected walk, your seat needs to 'contain' the walk a little more: your seat muscles close a little more at each stride to keep the walk steps short. You will feel as though you are rising through your diaphragm (without hollowing your back), using your body to raise your cob's centre of balance. Your hands maintain a lively bubbly contact, which has shortened a little, with slightly higher hand-carriage, asking gently for a more advanced collected outline. Your legs must, of course, maintain a lively impulsion despite the steps becoming shorter and shorter.

To move from collected walk into the diagonalized steps of piaffe, you simply adopt your piaffe position and aiding, and pulse with your legs until the diagonal steps emerge. Soon, you should be able to do this from a shoulder-in positioning, as this will not only put your cob into a 'sitting' position and lighten his shoulders further, but it will also keep his quarters under control. Again, for each of these steps, reward your cob as soon as you get what you want and remember to practise this on both reins and in different areas in the school.

Soon, transitions from the diagonalized half-steps of piaffe to the trot will help give the piaffe energy and keep it bubbling and popping like champagne. Ride two or three steps of piaffe before releasing the energy forward and trotting on. Again, build up these steps until you can ride four or five before releasing the piaffe forward into the trot.

PHOTO SEQUENCE BELOW
With many repeated rein-back to piaffe and then piaffe to trot transitions, you can develop a piaffe with increasing expression. Your cob cannot achieve this height of collection without a rider who is well balanced.

If your cob gets strong in your hand, go back to the rein-back, walk, rein-back transitions until he softens and his steps become more contained. If he rushes off in trot out of the rein-back, add some shortened walk steps and build up the diagonalized piaffe steps from there. If the initial bouncy piaffe steps peter out, ride every piaffe out into an energetic trot so your cob knows that energy is always a requirement. If his poll is carried low, lift both hands, expecting him to lift his head, and allow the piaffe steps to go a little more forward for a step or two. Although it is uncommon, some cobs will try to go hollow, in which case repeat your walk, rein-back, walk transitions with a focus on the round, soft outline before asking again for those diagonalized steps.

Jane showing a full piaffe on the spot.

As long as your cob does not show any of the faults mentioned above, you could start at this point to 'sit' him more on the spot for two or three steps before allowing the piaffe to cover a little ground again. At this stage, make sure he does not drop his poll or lose energy. If he does, following the advice given above should help.

Initially, the aiding of the legs will be slightly behind the girth, pulsing and energizing, urging your cob forward. Later on, as he becomes more conversant with the exercise, your lower legs begin to work alternately with the swing from side to side: as his hip drops and his belly swings away, your lower leg pulses and energizes. Having said that, you should not feel that you are putting lots of effort into the alternating pattern – rather your cob will allow it to happen naturally with the undulations of his body. Of course, he will only do this if he is truly forward and energetic without needing to be worked hard by you. When you feel as though your cob works himself off alternating legs, you can be sure his piaffe is developing well.

CHAPTER NINETEEN

Ridden Passage through Spanish Walk

Final Steps Forward

Passage is a movement that is often reserved for the purpose-bred sports horse but I have found that, if the piaffe is schooling well and is combined with the effects of the Spanish walk, the passage is not impossible for most cobs. Yes, they may find it difficult, but they should be able to give you a few passable steps, and you will find that, even if only a couple of full strides are being achieved, other work such as your cob's medium and extended trot will take on a new and more positive feel and balance.

PREREQUISITES

The prerequisites are as follows:

Cob's Prerequisites I feel it is essential that your cob is becoming established in piaffe before you start work on passage, although Spanish walk can be started sooner. It is important that the piaffe is started first because, if your cob learns the passage first, he could use these lofty steps as an escape from the 'sitting' requirements of the piaffe. Your cob should be happy to piaffe in-hand, give a couple of steps of Spanish walk and a couple of lofty trot steps in-hand through the influence of the Spanish walk.

Rider's Prerequisites Your posture and position must be close to correct, with an upright pelvis that does not tip to one side or the other. You should be able to maintain a steady, correct contact without pulling back or dropping the contact and therefore 'deserting' your cob. You should be well versed with piaffe and its aiding.

Spanish Walk

SEQUENCE OF DEVELOPMENT

Spanish walk has already been started in-hand (*see* Chapter 10). Its development ridden should follow a similar pattern to the in-hand work. Initially start at halt. Brush your cob's leg or shoulder with the whip and keep 'tickling' him until he responds by lifting his leg. Reward him for every attempt. Do this on both forelegs.

ABOVE LEFT Using the whip and a lifting rein to invite Ketchup to lift a foreleg.

ABOVE RIGHT Ketchup now lifts her other foreleg to a simple rein aid. The whip is no longer needed.

Once your cob offers a lifted leg from a quick brush or tickle of the whip along the shoulder or leg, you can start to lift the rein on the same side as you want your cob to lift his leg. Raise the rein, making an upward check down the rein at the same time as aiding with the whip. As before, every effort should be rewarded, and this should be done on both reins.

This can now be 'taken for a walk'. Initially, concentrate on one foreleg at a time. Walk on for a couple of strides, halt and then ask for the lifting of the leg, walk on again for a stride or two then halt and ask

'Taking it for a walk'.

for another lift of the same leg. Soon you will find the co-ordination necessary for you to make a leg lift, walk normally on the other three legs, before asking for the same leg to lift for its next stride. To co-ordinate this, keep the walk slow and apply your aid for the lifting of the leg as the shoulder is back on that side and ready to swing forward.

You can now begin to modify the way your cob reaches with his leg, rather in the same way as you did in-hand, though this should be easier ridden as it should already have been achieved in-hand. All you need to do is start to withhold your reward until a higher, loftier step with a straighter leg is offered. This is the moment at which you stop and reward your cob. You can even halt each time you ask for a lifted leg, and ask for the slightly higher, straighter leg, only giving the reward when that is achieved before moving on. The key here is to make the changes gradually, because if you try to make too big a change your cob will get confused. Think of a step 1cm higher than before, rather than expecting 10cm!

The next step is to keep the walk without any halting tendencies, and to lift the same leg each time it steps forward. Keep the walk slow and keep co-ordinating the aids with your cob's shoulder being back, so he has time to think about the lift and then to carry it out. Again, keep rewarding any good attempts made by your cob. This work should soon be achieved with each foreleg, on both reins, and, when that happens, your first full Spanish walk can be asked for, with consecutive lofty steps left and then immediately right.

It is at this point that all you need to do is co-ordinate the change from one leg to the other. This is easier if your cob is at the stage of responding to the rein aid rather than just the whip. If this is the case, ask for the lofty step from one foreleg, for example the right, just with the rein aid, and then immediately the other rein (in this case the left rein) can ask straight away. Coupling the rein aid for the second lofty step with the whip on the left-hand side will strengthen the aid for the Spanish walk step from the left leg. Building up consecutive steps of Spanish walk in this way ensures that the other foreleg follows through with the lofty stride straight after the first. Again reward, reward and reward! Now all you need to do is build up the Spanish walk steps from two to three, then four and slowly you will find that five or six steps are achievable.

Passage

SEQUENCE OF DEVELOPMENT

Only the beginnings of Spanish walk are necessary in order to start the passage though, as discussed, your cob must be fully conversant with the piaffe before passage is attempted.

Initially the build-up is as for the Spanish walk, the only difference being that your cob must be in a shortened slow trot rather than walk. So, to start with, ask your cob for a lofty step in walk on the leg that you will later be lifting in trot. Once he has given you a couple of leg lifts, ask for a transition to shortened trot and quite quickly ask your cob to lift the same leg again. The aid is given in time with the swing of the cob's belly and as the shoulder is swinging back so that he has time to think about what he needs to do and offer a response. A more sustained request to lift that leg may be needed, involving tapping his shoulder and upper leg with the whip until a slightly lofty step is felt. When this occurs, stop and reward him, as this is very difficult.

These individual steps on both reins should be repeated over time, and thought of progression should only be made when your cob consistently gives a lofty step each time he is asked for it on both legs and on both reins.

When this is in place you can ask for two consecutive steps in which your cob lifts the same leg. Again, proficiency in giving two consecutive steps on both legs and on both reins should be achieved consistently before further progression can be made. It is at this stage that you can start to incorporate the same rein aid as we used in the Spanish walk, because soon you will try to obtain your first left-right steps of passage and then the steps can be built up from there. Do not expect too many steps to string together too quickly; remember to build up slowly.

In Spanish walk, we were looking for a straightened, outstretched foreleg. For the passage, however, the leg should be folded, with bend in the knee. To achieve this, as we did in the Spanish walk, we wait for the flexed leg reaction and then we reward lavishly. This behaviour can be shaped from there. However, it has to be said that some horses of all types keep a slightly straighter leg than others in the passage; this tends to be conformational, and is related to the horse's natural movement. So, if your cob has plenty of knee action in his natural gaits, attaining a bent knee in the passage should not cause too much of a

Here I am building up to the passage in the same way as the Spanish walk, with a lifted rein and the use of my whip on Ketchup's shoulder. She knows what is requested of her.

RIGHT Building up the passage step by step. Here the tension is shown in Ketchup's mouth. The passage is hard work.

problem, whereas those that have a straighter, daisy-cutting action will tend to have straighter legs in their passage.

Transitions between Piaffe and Passage

Once your cob can give you a couple of lofty passage steps consistently, it is time to try a transition from the piaffe. This makes the passage 'sit' a little more. To achieve this transition, ask for a few steps of piaffe and then, when you are ready, use your cob's knowledge of the whip aid on his shoulder to initiate the first step of passage out of the piaffe. Your legs, while still a little behind the girth, move slightly in front of where they were for the piaffe. Keep your shoulders squared and allow your lower back to flex forward a little more, letting the stride step forward. Tapping on your cob's shoulder in the piaffe and then in the passage rhythm supports the passage and helps it to be maintained for a stride or two. Your body needs to stay with the movement and not get left behind in the transition, nor should it get too far forward, which can happen if you focus too much on the foreleg lifts. Initially, expect no more than one stride then release your cob forward into an easy working trot, and remember the all-important praise. This should be done on both reins and in a variety of places in the school. As you did with transitions from the shortened trot, build up the passage strides from the piaffe one at a time.

BELOW LEFT The moment of the transition from piaffe to passage.

BELOW RIGHT The piaffe encourages a more 'uphill', expressive and airborne passage.

Eventually, when your cob can make a transition from piaffe into passage and maintain it for five or six strides, you can then ask for a transition back to piaffe. To do this, your gluteals and inner thighs close in rhythm with the passage to shorten it. Your legs go back to your normal piaffe position, which is a little further back, and your fingers maintain a flexing feeling down both reins. You can make your body feel much more 'solid' to restrain the forward push of the passage, and lifting your diaphragm encourages the 'sit' of the piaffe.

These transitions between piaffe and passage are two of the hardest in equitation. Attempting them represents a huge journey in learning; achieving proficiency in them is the hallmark of classical dressage. Be very proud of your achievements.

Conclusion

'Dressage' nowadays has come to be almost synonymous with the competitive sport, and selective breeding over generations has produced warm-blooded horses that are built in a perfect balance for the modern sport and move ever more spectacularly. It should not be forgotten, however, that the true meaning of dressage is 'training' and, historically speaking, the horses and ponies being trained were not as highly bred as most seen nowadays in the dressage arena. Many of the dressage masters of the past worked specifically with rather ordinary horses and, indeed, some cobs. It is with horses like these that famous masters such as General Decarpentry achieved some of the most wonderful transformations. It remains the case, in the present day, that whatever our competitive ambitions may be, our 'ordinary' horses are just as worthy of high-quality training as any others, and will reward that endeavour. The cobs pictured in this book are proof not only that 'cobs can' but also that, using the progressive exercises set out in this workbook, your cob will not be limited by conventional mindsets.

In this book, as you have seen, the main themes throughout the schooling techniques and exercises are lightness and responsiveness. Cobs have many conformational advantages, such as strength, but many of the traditionally accepted methods of riding horses forward into unyielding contact would just be counterproductive with cobs. The techniques explained in this book ensure that your cob will use his chunky conformation in a positive, gymnastic way that will make him more rideable and manoeuvrable in a self-carriage that is uncommon in the mainstream equestrian world, especially where cobs are concerned.

The Cobs Can! Workbook can be usefully implemented to assist you and your cob into the higher levels of equitation. Sometimes it is our self-limiting beliefs that hold us back and, if this book helps to move readers beyond these beliefs, it has fulfilled its purpose. Sometimes, just attempting to school a more advanced movement opens up your experience to a whole other realm. Remember that sometimes progress needs a leap of faith, but with this book your leap of faith need not be in the dark. Attempting many of the more advanced movements and exercises will help inform the lower-level work so, while your aim may not be Grand Prix dressage, learning more advanced movements such as shoulder-in, travers or rein-back will help your cob become more supple in his Novice level work, improving bend, straightness and hind leg carrying capacity – and they will all be invaluable skills to enhance your hacking out in the countryside.

Index